Praise for Don McNair and
Editor-Proof Your Writing

"All writers, seasoned or newbie, should read, absorb, and put to use the lessons Don McNair offers."

—*New York Journal of Books*

"Don, I have to tell you that I'm VERY impressed with your book and already have a number of people in mind to suggest it to. Two of them are English teachers who are writing books and the others are writers I know. Kudos on compiling a book that is so engaging to be a resource book. I would have loved to have had this when I started. I love that you tell your readers to get 'professional editing' before a book goes out. I cringe at how many say 'I'm not spending for that' then expect to build a career in this business."

—*New York Times* best-selling author Dianna Love

"McNair offers great editing tips that will be sure to strengthen your manuscript!"

—*USA Today* best-selling author Cynthia Eden

Here's what aspiring writers say about Don McNair's "21-Step" approach to fog-free writing...

"Don, I have to take time out from editing my WIP to tell you how much I am enjoying your class. The information you give us is fabulous. I just counted the books I have purchased in the last twelve months dealing with writing. Twenty-seven! Twenty-seven books that have given me less usable information than your one class. Thank you. Thank you!"

—Linda Cousine, Aliso Viejo, CA

"I loved the class. For years people told me my writing wasn't clear, yet never explained why it wasn't. Your class explained why. I rate the class a 'ten.'"

—Charlotte Summers, Dallas, TX

"Thank you so much for this class. I learned a ton that I can even use in my day job of writing marketing copy, so it was sort of a two-fer."

—Linda Fletcher, Novi, MI

"This was the most detailed, spot-on, editing advice I've ever gotten, bar none. The lesson format conveyed a lot of information in a simple, elegant form. And you brought my attention to errors I was still making despite having taken other classes on the subject. I had no clue how many mistakes I was making. Once I picked my jaw up off the floor, I realized what a wake-up call you'd given me."

—Patricia Davis, Oakland, CA

"I LOVED this class. I wanted to let you know that this is, hands-down, the best class I've ever taken. It is immediately useful, and is taught logically and with enough examples that it is easy to see the problems in my own writing. Thank you so much for offering such a wonderful resource. I'm excited about looking at my WIP again! And, oh boy, can I see the difference after taking this class. Thank you!!!"

—Suzy Short, Richmond, VA

"I have mixed feelings about our class ending tomorrow. I've learned so much, and I don't want it to end! I started with a 105,600-word WIP, and have 'de-fogged' it down to 100,000. If this class went on much longer, I might be sitting here with a short story, instead of the next great American novel!"

—Capri Smith, Chesterfield, VA

"Your lessons helped me tremendously! I've actually re-opened a channel with a publisher, and your lesson on author intrusion is what made it possible. You're separating the men from the boys here, lemme tell ya. I have months of work ahead of me, but I can't wait to dig in."

—Debbie Robbins, St. John's, Newfoundland, Canada

"I used to make 30 passes trying to find the editing problems. Now, with your 21 Steps, I'm sooooooooo much more efficient. I can constantly refer back to examples to help me avoid each Step's traps."

—Leslie Randall, Palo Alto, CA

"Your '21 Steps' program is succinct, to the point, provides great examples and homework—it's excellent all the way around. I liked that I could work at my own speed, and wasn't inundated with 100 emails a day since my time is so limited. Thank you!"

—Louise Behiel, Calgary, AB, Canada

"I've learned boatloads in this course. The way your lessons communicate what to do and not do is very engaging, and your real-life examples bring it all home. Your teaching style is very effective, and I'm now applying a whole new lens to my writing. I've learned that the 200 pages I've written is just a working outline, and that those information dumps and backstories were my way of getting to know my characters. All that information was useful, but now it won't make it into the story."

—Melanie Martin, St. John's, Newfoundland and Labrador, Canada

"I just wanted to let you know that I've just sold *Catch Me a Catch*, the story we worked on in your class! This is my first novel, and I'd like to thank you for all the help and guidance that helped me get there."

—Sally Clements, Celbridge, County Kildare, Ireland

"I learned a great deal. You presented solid solutions to universal writing problems, and I definitely found my money and my time well spent! This course could very well make the difference between success for me and struggling along with the same old problems, getting nowhere. It's one thing to know what's wrong and quite another to know how to fix it."

—Susan Granade, Mobile, AL

"Thanks for a great class! I learned so many things that seem so obvious. I've read a lot of books on editing and writing, but this course showed the steps in a clear and concise way. You have given me direction and confidence in my editing process."

—Cici Edward, Chicago, IL

"Don's workshops are the best. His own writing is so CLEAN, a real pleasure to read. While some workshops are 'about,' Don's is a 'how-to.' He shares very specific techniques to clean up your own writing and provides handouts and exercises to identify your own brand of 'fog.' My standard for online workshops is what I have to show after I've completed the class. I can promise that Don's class is well worth the time and money."

—Rita Van Fleet, Mobile, AL

"I printed out your lessons and read them at bedtime. I have already made several edits to my WIP based on the information in your lessons. I have taken several online writing classes, and this is one of my favorites. I like your style!"

—Rita Garcia, Diamond Bar, CA

"I loved the course, and learned a lot about editing my own work. I edited the first three chapters of my WIP and they're much tighter (and shorter). I liked the format, the assignments, and being able to correct my work. Thanks for a great course that definitely improved my WIP and, hopefully, future books."

—Beverley Batema, Kelowna, BC, Canada

EDITOR-PROOF YOUR WRITING

21 Steps to the Clear Prose Publishers and Agents Crave

DON MCNAIR

Fresno, California

Editor-Proof Your Writing

To my wife Rita, the light of my life, the essence of my soul.

Published by Quill Driver Books
An imprint of Linden Publishing
2006 South Mary Street, Fresno, California 93721
(559) 233-6633 / (800) 345-4447
QuillDriverBooks.com

Quill Driver Books and Colophon are trademarks of
Linden Publishing, Inc.

ISBN 978-1-61035-178-2

135798642

Printed in the United States of America
on acid-free paper.

Library of Congress Cataloging-in-Publication Data

McNair, Don, 1938-
 Editor-proof your writing : 21 steps to the clear prose : publishers and
agents crave / Don McNair.
    pages cm.
 Includes bibliographical references and index.
 ISBN 978-1-61035-178-2 (pbk. : alk. paper)
 1. Authorship. 2. Editing. 3. Authorship--Marketing. I. Title.
 PN147.M476 2013
 808.02--dc23
                            2012049061

Contents

PART THREE: SHARING YOUR WORDS

INTRODUCTION

You *can* be published!

Unpublished writer "Barbara Stevens" asked me to critique and edit her newest unpublished novel's first chapter. "I've written twelve other manuscripts," she said, "and they've been rejected a lot of times. I hope you can figure out what's wrong."

Well, I did figure it out, and quickly. This lady was basically a good writer. Her blogs sparkled, she dreamed up creative plots, and her heart was certainly in her work. But she'd made a major craft mistake in that chapter and, presumably, in all twelve of those manuscripts. It was a mistake that almost guaranteed she'd never be published.

We discussed her problem (we'll get back to that later), and the light bulb over her head glowed brilliantly. She rewrote that first chapter and I edited it again, and, as if by magic, it became publishable. Barbara used her newfound knowledge to revise the rest of that manuscript, and then her twelve other novels. Within two months she sold one, and she's now been published many times. She's on her way.

The point? Barbara's breakthrough came directly from correcting that one craft mistake. She'd made it time and time again and was destined to repeat it again and again, until someone told her what it was.

You may be making that same mistake. Or, perhaps you're making another equally deadly one—mistakes we'll identify and resolve in this book—and are not aware of it. But there's hope.

Bad news, good news

If you've never been published, there's both bad news and good news.

The bad news is that most unpublished writers will *never* be published. Editors receive hundreds of manuscripts each week and ultimately buy fewer than one percent. We've all heard of hapless writers who have wall-papered their home or office walls with rejections. Perhaps you're one.

The reason is basic. Many writers send problem-riddled manuscripts to editor after editor, as Barbara did, believing they are perfect. In the meantime they blithely build the same flaws into their next manuscript. *They simply don't know they're making those mistakes.* Unless someone tells them or they somehow learn on their own, their manuscripts will be rejected the rest of their lives.

Note, however, that someone *does* recognize their problems. Those editors! They quickly spot them in a manuscript's first chapter—often on the first page—and reject the submission without reading further. They know the rest of the manuscript contains the same mistakes, just as we know an iceberg's submerged part is made up of more of the same ice seen on top. Editors simply don't have the time or inclination to teach authors writing skills. So they send out "sorry, it's not for us" letters and move on to the next manuscript in their bulging in-baskets.

The good news? That can change!

It's time for someone to tell these writers what they're doing wrong. And that, of course, is the purpose of this book. If you apply what you learn here to your current and future manuscripts, they'll be tremendously improved. Improved enough, perhaps, to entice that next editor to take you on.

I've seen your problems many times. I edited trade magazines for twelve years, supervised writers while writing for a major PR firm's national clients for six years, and headed my own company (McNair Marketing Communications) for twenty-two years. For the last five years I've run my own editing firm (McNairEdits.com), where I polish other writers' work. Believe me, I know firsthand the problems many writers build into their manuscripts. In my position of working through an editing network, I see hundreds of raw manuscripts, and most need substantial editing. What I see is what those experienced publishing editors and agents see, so I know why they reject ninety-nine percent of the manuscripts offered.

In those forty-plus years, I learned that most writers, particularly unpublished ones, need heavy editing. Unfortunately, most don't know they do. They haven't a clue. Their inappropriate and extra words seemed to act as a fog that slows car drivers down, or hides dangerous rocks from ship captains. The reader tries to navigate through the book, and if it's filled with unnecessary words and confusing information, she'll likely give up.

Although I enjoy the editing process, for years I secretly wished I could teach my writers to defog their own work. That, of course, seemed impossible.

But wait. I was wrong! That was before I discovered something that changed my own writing forever, and ultimately that of my clients. I'm betting it will change yours, too.

That personal revelation took place several years ago on a flight from Chicago to Atlanta, where I was to research an article for a client. Out of boredom, I was editing a fog-filled paperback, when I realized the same mistakes appeared over and over. I was intrigued. I bought another paperback at the Atlanta airport and edited it on the way home. A pattern emerged, and I became excited. Had I discovered the writer's Rosetta Stone?

Over the next several months, I edited many other paperback novels. I joined critique groups and aggressively edited other writers' fiction. I plowed through all those manuscripts from pre-published authors and the marked-up paperback books I'd tossed into a dresser drawer, and painstakingly sorted thousands of offending sentences and other problems by type. I eventually identified twenty-one distinct problems. Today I call their solutions, appropriately enough, the "21 Steps to Fog-Free Writing."

The inference staggered me. Just as there's a specific number of elements in chemistry's periodic table and letters in the alphabet, there's also a specific number of fog problems in writing. I realized many unnecessary words are actually tips of bad-writing icebergs, and that eliminating those words resolves otherwise complicated editing problems. In fact, *almost half of the 21 Steps actually strengthen action while shortening sentences.* You can see it happen right before your eyes.

So, here's the good news. You don't have to be an English major to achieve this writing miracle. You don't have to diagram sentences or study verb declensions, whatever they are. You don't have to learn complicated rules, wade through thick manuals of style, or immerse yourself in the technical mumbo jumbo of a book on editing. Applying what you learn here will make you a better writer than would struggling with any of those other options.

Here's why. Most editing manuals are like geography books that give great information about an area, but don't show you how to get from place to place. This book is a GPS that guides you through the writing wilderness to solve your *specific* writing problems.

Most editing manuals are like dictionaries from which you're asked to select words to write the Great American Novel. This book shows what specific words to use and what ones *not* to use.

This book is not loaded with theory. It instead presents knowledge one step at a time, and asks that you apply what you learned—one step at a time—to your Work-In-Progress's first chapter. You'll also edit a nine-chapter melodrama along the way, and you'll check your editing process against mine. When you've worked through this book, you'll have an editor-proof first chapter, and will be ready to edit the rest of your book. You'll learn how to write sparkling, clear, powerful copy that attracts readers, agents, and editors. And sales.

That's a pretty big claim, I realize. Just how do I expect you to accomplish that miracle?

First, consider your Work-In-Progress's first chapter—or the first chapter of that manuscript that constantly comes back from editors unwanted—as your battlefield. Incorporate what you learn in this book into that chapter, step-by-step, and it will become almost editor-proof.

You'll be surprised. Delighted. When you later apply the techniques to your whole manuscript, you'll watch it sparkle. And every manuscript you write from now on will be clearer and more compelling than any you've ever written, for two reasons: You won't make most of those mistakes in the first place, and you'll know exactly what to look for when you self-edit. You can find many of the problems simply by using your word processor's "find" function.

I've divided this book into three parts: *Part One: Putting Words In, Part Two: Taking Words Out,* and *Part Three: Sharing Your Words.* Part One deals with inserting information into the right place and in the right form as you write. Part Two deals with removing words that fog up your writing. That's where we put those 21 Steps to work. Part Three is about how to get your newly polished manuscript published and make all your work pay off.

So, consider this book as your doorway to better writing. Remember this old saying? "Give a man a fish, and he'll eat for a day, but teach him to fish, and he'll eat for a lifetime." Apply what you learn in this book, and you'll learn how to fish!

Thinking of self-publishing? Read this first.

If you're thinking about self-publishing your manuscript, you especially need to read this book.

That treasured manuscript of yours came back from publishers and agents several times, right? Well, maybe—just maybe—they knew what they were doing.

When you send them your work, you're actually taking part in a vetting process. If it's well written and fulfills their needs, editors and agents will probably send you a contract. Face it: If you keep getting it back, something basic may be wrong with your writing. You don't recognize the problems because you're the author, and self-editing one's own work is difficult. Your spouse doesn't see the problems because he/she loves you and is not a professional editor. Even your critique partners may not pick up on them. After all, they're probably also unpublished and may be making the same mistakes as you.

My advice? Have that manuscript edited professionally before sending it out. Have experienced eyes look it over and tell you what the problems are, and perhaps help you solve them.

At the very least—here comes the commercial—use this book as a guide to recognizing and resolving the problems yourself.

Now, let's get to work on your manuscript.

PART ONE

PUTTING WORDS IN

CHAPTER 1

Your classroom? It's your first chapter!

Chances are, you've already written a manuscript. Maybe you've shopped it around and even proudly wallpapered your house or apartment with the resulting rejection slips. What went wrong?

Well, you'll find out in this book.

Maybe, though, you've written only that first chapter. You know something's wrong with it but don't know what. That's okay, too. Again, you'll identify the problems while reading this book.

That first chapter is your classroom (think "battlefield") for learning the fiction-writing craft. All the basic mistakes you'll make throughout the total manuscript appear in it. Editors know that, and that's why they usually need only glance at the first chapter—often, only the first page or two—before rejecting a submission.

Jack M. Brickham, a well-known author and writing instructor, tells of being at a publishing house and peering into a room where editorial assistants were digging through an enormous slush pile looking for gold nuggets to pass on to the actual editors. He watched one young girl open a manila envelope, slip a manuscript out halfway, and glance at the top few lines of its first page. Within seconds she put it into its stamped, self-addressed envelope and tossed it into a voluminous "reject" pile.

She did this after reading only the first paragraph!

That last manuscript she rejected? Maybe it was *yours*. Your sweat, midnight hours, and dreams, not to mention the months and months of writing, saw the light of day for only seconds. Most of the nation's manuscript offerings are returned to their writers in this manner, with form rejection letters that say, in essence, "After careful consideration, we've had to pass on your thought-provoking story."

These form letters are bleak encouragement, to be sure. Editors don't want to hurt your feelings, but they simply don't have time to discuss your writing problems with you. So they send letters that give their recipients enough courage to send the same sample chapter(s) out again and again and to continue writing yet more unpublished—and unpublishable—novels.

The sad thing is, those new manuscripts will contain the same problems the first readers spotted in that first offering.

So, editors spot problems in your first chapter, often on the first page, in the first paragraph, or even the first sentence. That's why we use your first chapter as our classroom. I'll help you identify the problems that cause editors to return your manuscript virtually unread. More than that, I'll tell you how to fix those problems. At every step of the way, I'll ask you to use your newfound knowledge—right then and there—to improve your first chapter. When you've finished this book, you'll have a first chapter that will keep that editor reading, and, hopefully, he or she will request the full manuscript for review. Of course, you'll want to give the rest of your manuscript the same careful attention you gave your first chapter before you send it out.

YOUR ASSIGNMENT

Many newbies use strange fonts, single spacing, and other visual tricks, unknowingly guaranteeing that editors will spot them as neophytes. So your first assignment is to present your work in a professional manner. While there are slight variations, the format I describe below is universally accepted.

First, copy your manuscript's first chapter into a new file called "First Chapter" (or whatever you want to call it) and format it as follows:

1. Set the margins at one inch, all around.
2. Select Times New Roman (or Century) as your font.
3. Using your word processor's numbering command, insert "1" in the upper right corner of your first page. The rest of the pages will be automatically numbered.
4. Select "header," and type in your last name, a forward slash, and all or part of your title flush left. If you want, select boldface for both this and the page number (which is now on the same line, at the right margin).
5. Select "double space" for the body copy.

6. Hit the "enter" key eight times.
7. Type "Chapter 1" over the body copy, center it, and boldface it.
8. Double space after "Chapter 1" and begin to enter your body copy in regular type (not boldface or italic).

Do these instructions seem fussy? Trust me, they're not! A manuscript boasting clean, competent formatting assures an editor that at the very least the writer knows the basics about how the publishing industry works.

Now, let's create a title page for your manuscript. Put your name, address, phone number, and email address on separate, single-spaced lines in the upper left corner of a blank page, much as you would list your contact information in a business letter. Then drop one-third down the page, set your auto-indentation to "center," and type your manuscript's title in all caps. Type your word count in the upper right-hand corner, also in caps, like this: WORD COUNT 78,500.

That's it! Let's move on to Chapter 2.

CHAPTER 2

Why you should be a hooker

Okay, let's get started on that first chapter of yours. It will actually be your workbook, and from this point on you'll refer to it often. You'll rework it, lesson by lesson, Step-by-Step, to make it virtually editor-proof.

At the end of most chapters and Steps in this book, I'll ask you to re-edit your first chapter, armed with the knowledge you've just gained. When you finish this book, assuming you've done the things asked of you, you'll have a sparkling first chapter that will entice even the most hardhearted editor. In order to measure progress—and to assure you're not afraid to experiment—you'll need to copy your first chapter into its own file. If you haven't done that yet, I'll wait here for you to do so.

Waiting, waiting, waiting…

Ready? Here we go.

Your first hook

Why did that publisher or agent reject your last manuscript? The problem could be that you simply didn't use a good "hook" to engage her. The title of this very chapter is a hook. Didn't it make you want to read further?

Remember the publishing house's first reader who didn't even take the manuscript from its envelope? She slipped it out halfway, glanced at the first paragraph, and tossed it into the reject pile. As cruel as that sounds, wasn't she doing the same thing you do when you visit a bookstore?

If you're a typical book buyer, you select a book in your preferred genre that has an appealing front cover. You read the back-cover blurb and, if it interests you, you open to the first page and read the first few sentences. If they don't "hook" you—that is, make you want to read more—you replace that book on the shelf and move to the next one.

That's exactly what that publishing house's first reader did. We can't really blame her, can we? She knows what book buyers are looking for—a book that grabs and holds their interest.

Knowledgeable writers make it virtually impossible for readers to put their book down by starting their story with a hook: a sentence that asks a story question the reader wants answered. Following are examples from published novels of several genres.

> *Morgan Turner squinted up at Captain Montgomery's counting room, which was, as promised, the last office in a long, tall brick building—last office, last hope.*
>
> *Wicked Woman*, by Denise Eagan

What does she mean, "last hope?" Why is Ms. Turner visiting this Captain Montgomery, whoever he is? How can he help her? Notice the author has posed questions readers want answered. To find those answers, they have to keep reading.

Here's another example of a good opening hook:

> *It will all be over soon.*
>
> *Magic Hour*, by Kristin Hannah

Good lord! What will be over soon? And who is it this—this unknown thing—is happening to? Even the most jaded editor will read on to find out.

Another example:

> *She flew in at night, in a small private plane that she'd chartered using the last of her cash.*
>
> *The Sicilian's Virgin Bride*, by Sarah Morgan

Wow! It looks like this girl's in trouble. Night…chartered airplane… last of her cash…can you put this book down without reading ahead to find out what's going on? I bet not. The reason is, of course, the hook.

Another:

> *Brad Ballivan opened the driver's side door of the waiting pick-up truck, tossed his guitar inside and turned to wave farewell to the pilot and crew of the private jet he hoped never to ride in again.*
>
> *The McKettrick Way*, by Linda Lael Miller

The character is apparently a cowboy returning home. But from where? Why was he riding a private jet? And why, pray tell, did he not want to do that again?

The above hooks were from romance novels, but similar hooks are used in every fiction genre. Here are examples from mystery novels:

Death wasn't normally on my mind in the grocery store parking lot.
                    Murder in the Milk Case, by Candice Speare Printice

Who of us could stop reading after that first sentence? We know the character's in a parking lot, and someone's died, but who? What are the circumstances?

Why was an L hanging in the window?
                              Worth Its Weight in Old, by K. D. Hays

That's a great hook. The author poses the question, then answers it in the next paragraph. But there's yet another hook waiting for us there, and so we're off on a wild read, chasing even more hooks.

Something about the Out of Time antique store didn't feel quite right that Tuesday afternoon.
                         Murder on the Ol' Bunions, by S. Dionne Moore

We know something's wrong, but what? Well, it has to do with an antique shop, but—and we read on, to find out what's happening.

Why would someone run down a young woman and not stop?
                              Murder by Proxy, by Suzanne Young

An excellent question, is it not? Don't you want to read on to find out? Here are examples from science fiction novels:

As far as Dee Daniels was concerned, too many idiots with death wishes filled the world.

                              I'll Be Slaying You, by Cynthia Eden

Something major has happened to make the point-of-view character think this. What was it? How will it affect the character's day?

Water. Valkerie Jansen forced one foot in front of the other, a weary survivor on a death march across a dry and barren planet.

The Fifth Man: A Science Fiction Romantic Suspense Mars Adventure,
by John B. Olson and Randy Ingermanson

Those two sentences set up the story well. Why's there just one man? Why is it a death march? Why is he on a dry and barren planet?

We've seen romance, mystery, and science fiction hooks, but I emphasize that hooks are important in *any* fiction genre. To see good hooks, simply go to Amazon.com and find books on your genre. Click on a book's image (it says "Click to Look Inside" above it), and read the first lines of the sample chapter shown.

If you're still confused about what a hook is, think about the little old lady who goes to bed promptly at ten thirty. A little old man in the apartment above her goes to bed at ten thirty-five. She lays there listening as he drops his first shoe, then the second. With a smile, she rolls over and falls asleep.

But what would happen if that little old man dropped the first shoe, then quietly placed the second one on his nightstand? Our little old lady would still be lying there wide awake, wouldn't she? She'd be staring into the darkness at the ceiling, perhaps as her heart races a bit, waiting for that second shoe to drop.

It's your job, as an author of fiction, to drop that first shoe, *and wait before your drop the second.*

We saw examples of good hooks (first shoes) above. Let's now look at an example of a manuscript's opening paragraph that does not start with a hook, but certainly needs one:

It was a late spring afternoon in Nebraska. The grove next to the Platte River was alive with chirping birds. The cottonwood trees stood proudly, exhibiting their limbs laden with green, unopened seeds. Armed with her sketchbook, charcoal, and a wooden water bucket, Anne approached the river where oft a herd of deer came to drink. Easily concealed in her drab gingham dress, she walked to the river's edge. Hearing the unexpected sound of splashing water, she frowned. Peering from behind a tree, she gaped at the site.

There, in the middle of the river surrounded by hip-high crystalline water, stood a Greek statue come to life, just like the ones she had seen in the books in her father's trunk on the wagon. And what a magnificent view it was. There was no comparison between them, though. This was finely sculpted flesh and...

If you were a publisher's first reader, would you get past this deadly opening? As a casual book buyer in a store, would you take this book home? Probably not.

But note, however, that the second paragraph contains the seed of an excellent first-line hook, which could read this way:

Good heavens. A naked man was standing in the river!

I'm a male. But I have to tell you... when I see that naked man standing in that river, I get excited.

I get excited because I wonder what he's doing there. I get excited because I'm anxious to find out what happens next. (By the way, that writing sample has other problems we'll discuss in another chapter.)

Sometimes, of course, the hook won't handily fit into one sentence. That's okay, if it *starts* in that first sentence, as the one below does. It's from my novel *Mystery on Firefly Knob* (see the Appendix for details on those of my novels which I use as examples in this book):

Erica Phillips blinked, moved the registered letter closer to the desk lamp, and re-read it:

Dear Miss Phillips:

This is to inform you that your recently deceased father, Eric Lee Emerson, has willed you property overlooking the Sequatchie Valley southeast of Crossville, Tennessee...

She dropped the letter to her lap. Now that made no sense at all. Her father was Paul Phillips, and he died in an auto accident four years ago!

Ah! We have a puzzle. The situation is impossible, of course. Unless—unless—unless what? The reader reads on to answer that question.

The mid-scene hook

A hook may get those elusive readers past the first paragraph, but what keeps them reading the whole scene? Why, more hooks, of course.

Remember that story about our little old lady? If the little old man upstairs immediately drops that second shoe, she's off the hook (pun intended) and can turn over and go to sleep. You don't want that to happen in your story. You want to constantly keep your reader on the edge, to continue anticipating what's coming next.

You want to drop that first shoe, then wait a while before dropping the second. *But before you drop that second shoe, you want to drop the first shoe of another pair.* You want to keep those readers staring at the proverbial ceiling by continually dropping first shoes until they finish your book, perhaps at three o'clock in the morning. Always keep them anxious to find out what happens next.

Let's look at some examples.

At the opening of my first novel, *The Long Hunter*, a young, orphaned boy living in the 1770s on the Virginia frontier is cleaning tables at a pioneer inn. The reader quickly realizes something major has occurred that put the boy into this situation, but what? Answering that question would be dropping the second shoe. But before I drop it, I say this:

Sweat dropped onto his chin, more prominent now than when he'd arrived two weeks ago, before he'd lost the weight.

Before he'd lost the weight? What's that all about? Why did he lose it? And why did he come here two weeks ago? Something major has happened to this poor boy, but what?

So, the reader keeps reading.

I put those five words *(before he'd lost the weight)* into the story to keep our readers on edge, to create uncertainty in their lives. They'll continue reading until they find out why he lost that weight and what happened two weeks ago, and then they'll put the book down, and…

No, they won't!

They won't because before we drop the second shoe by telling them what happened to our hero, we'll drop a first shoe from another pair. And we'll continue playing this shoe-dropping game throughout the book.

Let's take another example of a mid-scene hook, this one from my young adult novel, *Attack of the Killer Prom Dresses*. In the opening paragraph, our heroine and her boyfriend are picking up a "TV-sized box" from a store. That's the first shoe. What on earth could be in that box?

As they put it into the car, we see this:

"Careful there," she said. "You break this thing, my whole life's down the tubes."

WHY YOU SHOULD BE A HOOKER

Wow! What could be in that box that's so important? (Well, she's a teenage girl, so it could be anything at all, but that's not the right answer.) So the readers' curiosities are piqued, and they read on to answer that question. Notice we haven't dropped the second shoe yet. We've simply picked up the first one and waved it once more in the readers' faces.

The end-of-scene hook

Readers tend to lay a book down when they've finished a scene or chapter. Everything's been neatly tied up, and, in a way, the next scene or chapter starts another adventure. Your job as a writer is to keep your reader from pausing when they reach this point. How? By using a hook that forces them to leap over the gap into the next scene or chapter.

Although you may not have been aware of it, you see this little trick pulled every day on TV. Consider, for example, the once-popular TV program "Deal or No Deal." The contestant has selected a briefcase with a hidden amount of money inside, and we're anxious to find out how much it is. As we sit there in anticipation, Howie Mandell turns to the camera and says, "We'll find out how much is in the briefcase…after this word from our sponsors." So, we hang around through the commercial—just like we read on into the next scene or chapter in a skilled writer's book—to make sure we don't miss that vital information.

Another example is found in "The Biggest Loser," where members of two or more teams are weighed to see which team must vote a member out. The competition is close, the last fat person is standing on the scales, and various numbers flash on its display. Ah, we'll soon find out what team is going to—no, not yet!

As those numbers flash, the camera pans and shows surprised looks on the other contestants' faces. The music builds to a crescendo and we go to commercial. It's very effective, don't you agree? Won't you be right back after you've gotten that drink?

That's what you must do at the end of every chapter. You must put a hook in, snag the readers' attention, and build their anticipation so high that they literally have to read into the next scene or chapter to find out what happens.

Let's again consider some examples from my book, *The Long Hunter*.

In Chapter 1, our young hero, Matt McClaren, is at an inn run by the mean innkeeper. An old, inebriated farmer named Dandridge comes in and sees Matt's unfortunate situation and announces he's taking Matt home. The innkeeper flashes a pistol and says if the old man tries to take Matt, he'll kill them. Here's the scene's ending:

Dandridge's hand guided Matt to the door. He stumbled, and Matt felt his weight as they stepped outside. The cold wind hit him, and he shivered as he fought his chilling sickness. He walked rigidly, braced for a bullet. He heard a click, then a pop behind him. The stars swirled, and he hit the ground.

My goodness. That mean innkeeper killed Matt! No, he couldn't have; isn't the young boy the book's hero? But still…

And the reader reads on, into the next chapter.

Flipping through the pages, we see hooks at the end of every chapter. Here's a sampling:

He looked at the door where an angry Struthers had disappeared, and felt a chill. He had a feeling they'd not heard the last of that man.

Reader: When will that Struthers person return? What will happen to poor Matt?

He took one long look east toward Fincastle, wondered if the sheriff had found Struthers' body yet, then shuddered and turned back west.

Reader: Ah, there's something else I must worry about. When the sheriff finds the body, will he come after poor Matt?

"Well… well, maybe. But I tell you what. I ain't goin' to hold your hand. You don't pull your load, you just hike on down the trail. Now, you get out of those wet clothes 'fore you catch your death."

Reader: Goodness! Will poor Matt pull his load? Or will this new character abandon him in the wilderness?

Matt looked north once more, then forced himself to turn away, toward Virginia. There was danger in both places. There might even be danger where he was standing.

Reader: Danger where he's standing? Why, yes—he's surrounded by Indians. Winter's coming, and he's alone in the wilderness with only a handful of powder and bullets. Oh, my goodness, what's going to happen?

YOUR ASSIGNMENT

Okay, you're ready to improve your first chapter (and ultimately your whole manuscript).

Remember: Your assignments in this book aren't make-work exercises. They're designed to help you, step-by-step, upgrade your work to where an editor will be eager to offer you a contract. But for that to happen you have to put in the effort.

You did make a copy of your first chapter, right? And, you've formatted it to follow publishing industry standards? Good! Then let's get going:

First, rearrange your chapter's opening page to get a major hook into the first paragraph, preferably the first sentence. On a separate piece of paper, write down the specific story questions your hook presents. (If you can't do this, you don't actually have a hook.)

Put at least two hooks into your chapter's middle, more if you can. Keep dropping those first shoes! Again, write down the story questions asked by the hooks.

Rework each scene's last paragraph to include a hook that forces the reader to read into the next scene. Once again, identify the questions which will keep that reader reading.

CHAPTER 3

What's your point of view?

Point-of-view (POV) characters are those whose mind we are in. We see what they see, feel what they feel, and experience what they experience. The only information we get is through their senses, as revealed by what they say and think. In this chapter, we'll discuss three points of view: first person, third person, and omniscient (bird's-eye). I'll also suggest yet another POV, one which you may never have heard of before. (Notice the mid-scene hook?)

First-person POV

With first-person POV, the characters are talking with us in real time, telling us what they see and do as they see and do it. An example:

> I walked into the bar, and Brad looked up from his drink. "About time," he said.
> I didn't say anything, but sat down. I figured I'd take his crap for a few minutes, then tell him what really happened to the letter.

Some writers and publishers think this POV is confining and tend not to use it. Readers can learn only what the POV character actually experiences and can soon become bored by the confined perspective. Authors, on the other hand, can run into problems as they work to flesh out their stories.

Third-person POV

By far, the most common POV used by authors is "third person," written in the past tense. Here's an example:

When Betty walked into the bar, Brad looked up from his drink. "About time," he said.

She didn't say anything, but sat down. She figured she would take his crap for a few minutes, then tell him what really happened to the letter.

Notice this passage is written in Betty's POV. The big clue is the last sentence, where there is no question that we're in her mind, listening to her thoughts, known as "internal dialogue," a fancy term meaning the POV character's thoughts. As a writer, you want your reader to think with the character's mind, see through her eyes, and react through her other senses.

For example, what would happen if Brad sat back into his chair onto a prankster's tack? He'd yell out, wouldn't he? But since we are in Betty's POV, not his, we wouldn't feel it. We could write that action something like this:

Brad sat back into his chair and jumped up, screaming.

Oh, my God! Betty jumped up too, her heart racing. What on earth had happened?

Since we're in Betty's POV, not Brad's, we have no idea what happened to the poor guy. But we do know its effect on Betty. She jumps up, her heart races, and she's confused. We must wait until Brad tells Betty (and us) why he suddenly jumped up as he did.

One of the most telling mistakes new writers make is to "head hop;" that is, they frequently jump from one person's mind to another's, perhaps like this:

Brad sat back into his chair and jumped up, screaming. He realized a jokester had put a tack in his chair, and the damned thing hurt like hell.

Oh, my God! Betty jumped up too, her heart racing. What on earth happened?

Brad looked around. Who'd done it? He vowed to himself to find out, and fast.

See what we've done? We've head-hopped from Brad, to Betty, and then back to Brad. If that editor somehow got this far and sees this faux pas, she'd surely hurl the manuscript into the reject pile. An experienced author may occasionally use the third-person omniscient POV for effect, but when it's used inconsistently by a new writer it becomes a major red flag for editors.

Conventional wisdom says to stay in one POV for at least an entire scene. You say you've seen published books that changed POV more often? Maybe so. But it was probably done by an experienced, well-published writer who knows the rules as well as how to break them for effect. My advice? Wait until at least your tenth published novel before trying it yourself.

Omniscient POV

The omniscient, or bird's-eye, POV was popular many years ago. It has the effect of God looking down on his human creatures and knowing what each is thinking. So, as the novel progressed, we jumped from one character's head to another's, somewhat like in the example above. Often, this God-like narrator also talked directly to the readers, saying things like, "And now, dear readers, unknown to little Bess, the strange man…"

Some authorities say this POV is dead. I think it is not. It unfortunately lives on in another guise, causing editors to toss rejected manuscripts every which way. What I'm talking about could logically be called *Author's POV*. It's something writers must constantly guard against. I'll go into more detail on this phenomenon in the next chapter. (See the chapter-ending hook?)

YOUR ASSIGNMENT

Read all internal dialogue in your first chapter to make sure your POV is clear and consistent and that you don't "head hop" within scenes.

CHAPTER 4

Don't be an information dumper

You have two choices. Write in the "here and now" or dump information. I'll tell you right now that editors and agents want you to write in the "here and now."

Unpublished writers often present information dumps, sometimes in the form of backstories, in their manuscripts. How do you recognize one? Generally, in the midst of an information dump, your characters don't *do*, they *think*. They think as they drive a car. As they sit in their office. As they ride an elevator. Nothing of interest happens in real time. If your critique partner tells you your story actually starts on page seven, she's saying that the first six pages are an information dump, and the live action starts on page seven. Those six pages generally include information you think the reader needs in order to understand your characters, but the way it's organized makes the reading process a dull experience.

Remember the story about Barbara Stevens in the introduction? Her whole first chapter was an information dump. It opened as the main character sat at her office computer trying to decide if she wanted to answer the email of an ex-girlfriend who had stolen her boyfriend two years before. As we're locked into her mind through POV, we're exposed to the whole sordid story that took place then. What is the only live action in that twenty-six page chapter? Well, our character thinks at her computer, walks out to her car, drives home, and enters her apartment. That's it.

However, a lot of exciting things happened to Barbara's character two years earlier. Heart-rending, tear-jerking things. But we weren't *shown* them. We were only *told* about them—two years later. At my suggestion, Barbara rewrote that chapter, putting those past events into real time. The result was a snappy start that's so full of action the reader can't help but want to read more.

Your own novel will be much more interesting if you *show*, instead of *tell*. In fact, editors who do read past your manuscript's first paragraph stop reading when they're *told* too much and don't *see* enough action. Unfortunately, many writers who hear the "show-don't-tell" advice don't really understand what it means.

When writers *tell* instead of *show*, they're generally making the mistake of writing the story from the *author's POV*, and not the characters'.

Let me give you a before-and-after example from my own work years ago. The first version, written in the author's POV, read like this:

> *But the site itself had been inhabited for much longer. The previous day she and Mike had jogged along an old path which edged the Knob, and she spotted the stark, vertical rock chimney of a burned-out cabin. It jutted from a weathered rock foundation which was now covered with thick vines and forest debris. The cabin had been built near the Knob's edge, which plummeted almost two thousand feet to the valley floor. When that one-room cabin was built, its owner had probably cleared trees away to open the valley up for a spectacular view.*

Notice that the author is telling about the discovery, just as one tells ghost stories around a family campfire. There is no action. There was action yesterday, but that doesn't count as action today.

I thought that excerpt was fine writing until an old writing pro pointed out the problem. I read it again, and—by gosh, she was right. What follows is the passage as I rewrote it to put the scene into a *character's* POV and *show* the action, instead of leaving it in the *author's* POV and *telling* about it:

> *Mike stepped aside and she saw a clearing. Grass, kept at bay in the deep woods they'd passed through, covered an area the size of an average yard.*
>
> *"This is it?" she asked.*
>
> *"Yep. The original cabin site. See if you can find it."*
>
> *She saw nothing but the trees and grass. Blue sky appeared over a huge, waist-high stone outcropping at her left.*
>
> *"Why, we're right at the bluff's edge," she said.*
>
> *"That's right. Jump off that rock, and you'll fall almost two thousand feet."*

And then she saw the vertical stone chimney. She'd overlooked it before, since it resembled the surrounding tall trees. She stepped tentatively toward it. As her eyes adjusted, she saw the stone foundation of a long-gone, one-room cabin. Its chimney rose from one corner, its hearth opening toward the center. Slanting rays filtering through the treetops brought the chimney and foundation to life.

She turned to Mike. "Look at that—it's just like a shrine. Why, I feel like I've just stepped out of a time machine."

The secret is to always write in real time. Use backstory information only as needed, where needed, and in context. Don't *tell* what happened in the past, but *show* it as part of the action now. You'll find that, although it can be useful research for the writer, most of the backstory information is not needed in the final story.

Bad, better, and best

As you write fiction or edit what you've already written, think of the information you present as being at one of three levels: bad, better, or best. Then upgrade that information as best you can.

The "bad" level has information told from the author's POV, as in the first example above. The revealed events happened in the past. There is no action today. There is little or no dialogue. Here's another example:

After she ate her sandwich, Mary left the dance without answering Brad's questions about the Pekinese.

See? No action, no dialogue. The author is telling us about something that happened in the past. A scene or chapter written at this level could have a bored editor flinging a submitted manuscript across the room.

The "better" information level—and it's not really much better—at least presents thoughts from the POV of a live human being. Here's an example:

Jane started her Mazda and pulled out into the traffic. That Mary, she thought with disgust. She ate her sandwich and simply left the dance. She should have at least answered Brad's questions about the Pekinese.

This is hardly polished writing, but at least we have human involvement. Although the information Jane's thinking is still dead and has no action, we do see Jane. In small, well-placed doses, using such internal

19

dialogue is an acceptable way to pass information. Unfortunately, some authors use this approach for pages and pages, and the only live action we have is the heroine doing the equivalent of driving that car. It's easy to see why so many manuscripts are rejected.

Okay, we've discussed the "bad" and the (not much) "better" ways to present information. Now, let's look at the "best."

When you start a new book, there's certain information you may feel you must reveal. Rather than have the author tell us about it, or have a character think about it, have the heroine confide the information to a sidekick in real time, perhaps like this:

> *Jane set her margarita on the bar and turned to Amy, who stared at her pocket mirror as she adjusted her hair. "Did you see that?"*
>
> *Amy looked up. "See what?"*
>
> *"Mary. She just ate her sandwich and left."*
>
> *Amy glanced at the lit ballroom exit, past entwined couples dancing cheek to cheek on the dimly lit dance floor. "Wow. Well, did she answer Brad's questions about the Pekinese?"*
>
> *"I don't think so."*
>
> *Jane frowned, and retrieved her drink. She brought it to her lips and tasted the bitter salt, looked around, and paused. Standing by a small table, lit only by its flickering candle, was Brad, staring at the entrance.*
>
> *"She should have, you know?" Jane sipped again, and set her drink down. "After all, Brad was kind enough to have the Pekinese fixed."*

I'll admit I got carried away with that last example, but I did so with purpose. Didn't you feel like you were there, watching this scene play out? Didn't you catch the action—Amy primping, Jane sipping and tasting, dancers dancing, and perhaps even Brad frowning? Didn't you get the feeling that all this is happening now, and that you are on hand watching the scene unfold? This give-and-take is important. It keeps readers engaged. If you write in this mode, they'll continue to read your novel.

YOUR ASSIGNMENT

Okay, now it's time to identify your deadly *tell* writing so you can change it to *show* writing. Ready?

With your word processor's highlighter, highlight every "author's POV" passage in your first chapter. If you have difficulty recognizing the problem in your own work, ask a writer friend to read the "Don't be an information dumper" chapter you're reading now, then read your writing and identify areas that need work. Be sure to tell her not to critique the work, but to only identify what's there (the exercise will probably improve her writing, too).

Later we'll do something about those author-POV passages you identify.

CHAPTER 5

Your manuscript is a Christmas tree

It's easy for me to tell you to get rid of your information dump and to ramble on about eliminating the author's POV and so on, but just how do you do it? How do you get all that information into the proper places? And, for heaven's sake, just where are the proper places?

Well, think of your manuscript as a Christmas tree.

Let's say you've just brought a new Christmas tree into your home. It looks weird, doesn't it? At this point, it's only a piece of vegetation you've dragged in and erected in front of the window.

But now the fun starts. You get your box of antique ornaments from the attic and go to work. You string the lights, perhaps throw on some tinsel, and hang those ornaments, the smallest ones at the top. That star tree-topper your grandmother bought in New York the weekend she met your grandfather? You lovingly take it from its well-worn box and place it just so on the tree's tip. And the handmade ornaments your kids presented you after creating them in grade school years ago? Why, they go right at the front, at eye level.

When you're finished and step back to admire your work, you realize that tree is now much more than vegetation dragged in from the forest or mall. It represents a part of your life. It brings back memories of past Christmases, of past lives.

Your manuscript works just like that tree.

Let's say you've completed it and stand back to look it over. You realize something is wrong. You've spotted an information dump—think of it as ornaments bunched up together, looking cluttered and odd—and you know you need to work the information into the story.

But how?

First, identify the "dump" information's important elements (individual ornaments). Then search your manuscript—that tree—for a good place to attach them.

Here's an example of what I mean. As you'll recall from Chapter 2, my book *Mystery on Firefly Knob* starts this way:

Erica Phillips blinked, moved the registered letter closer to the desk lamp, and re-read it:

Dear Miss Phillips:

This is to inform you that your recently deceased father, Eric Lee Emerson, has willed you property overlooking the Sequatchie Valley southeast of Crossville, Tennessee....

She dropped the letter to her lap. Now that made no sense at all. Her father was Paul Phillips, and he died in an auto accident four years ago!

As we discussed then, this opening includes a strong hook. But I wanted it to work even harder.

Our heroine, Erica Phillips, has just lost her antiques business site to urban renewal. She has to find a new home for her business within sixty days or she *has* no business. The whole story before us is based on her searching for that home in the face of major conflicts.

I could have had Erica stew about this problem in a backstory before she receives the registered letter. Or, I could have stopped the story action later and had her think about the no-business-home problem. But as I searched my Christmas-tree/manuscript, I saw the perfect place to "hang the ornament." I added it immediately after the above-quoted material, like this:

She peered at the letter. Its address stared back in all its gold-embossed glory. A chill ran down her spine just as it had when she'd received another registered letter a month before, giving her ninety days to move her antiques out of the old house. Or, she presumed, they'd be carted off to the dump along with the building.

Note that we've attached that ornament to the tree *in context*, like we put your children's handmade ornaments in their proper front-and-center location. Both the letters were registered. The character is making an association. Now Erica doesn't have to sit thinking about the problem, and we readers don't have to be bored reading several paragraphs of ancient history. Later on, when she acts on finding a new place, we'll already know why.

Let's take another example, this one from *The Long Hunter*, a novel we discussed in Chapter 1. In the story, young Matt McClaren's parents are massacred by Indians and he goes to an inn for help. The cruel innkeeper keeps him as a virtual slave. The story opens two weeks later at the inn, where drunken farmer Dandridge is present. Dandridge, as you'll recall, will take Matt home with him.

I pondered what was the best way to present the "massacre" information? Where should I hang that ornament on my manuscript tree?

I had several options. First, I could have opened the novel from the author's POV, with that unseen narrator telling the massacre story. Or, I could have told the story in a separate scene that showed the event taking place. Another possibility? I could have had Matt think about the event two weeks after it happened—and stop the story's action in the process—as he cleaned tables at the inn. After considering these possibilities I realized there was a fourth option: I could let the innkeeper tell the story. And that's what I did.

Here's how the passage came out:

"Well, it's hard to believe." Struthers sighed and pulled another towel from under the bar. He slowly wiped the surface. "You'd think this here valley was gettin' civilized. Hell, we been living here a while, at least up in the north part. But it ain't civilized at all, no siree."

He bent forward and squinted hard at Matt. The crowd quieted. Struthers' gaze drifted from Matt to his bar customers. He let the silence build, as if he enjoyed the attention.

"Well, I was standin' right here, and that there boy come runnin' in. He must be…what, fourteen, fifteen years old? But he was cryin' like a baby. Said the Indians killed his daddy and run off with his mama and sister. Next morning some militia took him back up there and found the Indian camp up on the Jackson River."

His voice rose during the story's telling, and the crowd quieted more. Matt gathered three trenchers and carried them down the table, dodging among staring patrons. His ears burned, his face was hot. Struthers now stood erect, palms planted solidly on the bare bar before him, boring his gaze into Matt's soul.

"Them Indians was already gone," he said. "But they found the boy's mama. She was layin' there deader'n hell, stripped naked."

Look at all I accomplished by doing this. The massacre became a part of the inn scene's action. The hero lived the exciting story again, in front of the reader and the inn customers. The innkeeper revealed his character to the reader (I didn't have to *tell* the reader he was a bad man; I let the character himself *show* it). Now the old farmer had something to react to. And, as author, I was able to more fully develop the setting.

Make facts a part of the action

You've just seen how easy it is to put whole hunks of information into context in your manuscript. Well, it's equally easy to insert descriptive story objects.

Do you remember the story hook about the naked man standing in the river (Chapter 2)? In it, the author had an unseen narrator (the author's POV) set the scene by describing various objects in a catalogue-like manner. I'm repeating it below so you can easily understand the edited version that follows it:

It was a late spring afternoon in Nebraska. The grove next to the Platte River was alive with chirping birds. The cottonwood trees stood proudly, exhibiting their limbs laden with green, unopened seeds. Armed with her sketchbook, charcoal, and a wooden water bucket, Anne approached the river where oft a herd of deer came to drink. Easily concealed in her drab gingham dress, she walked to the river's edge. Hearing the unexpected sound of splashing water, she frowned. Peering from behind a tree, she gaped at the site.

There, in the middle of the river surrounded by hip-high crystalline water, stood a Greek statue come to life, just like the ones she had seen in the books in her father's trunk on the wagon. And what a magnificent view it was. There was no comparison between them, though. This was finely sculpted flesh and…

Let's rework that information to make the mentioned objects a part of the action—a part of what we are *seeing*—rather than part of what we are *told* about. Here's one way to do that:

Good heavens. A naked man was standing in the river!

Anne dropped her sketchbook, charcoal, and bucket, and backed quickly into the seed-laden cottonwood trees. She hoped her drab gingham dress would help conceal her from the man, and silently cursed the loud chirping birds which could give her away. She again gazed out into the river...

You'll recall that the narrator also informed us, as an unattached fact, that deer often came to sip from the river. Well, let's also make that a part of the action, by adding this:

Two deer backed away from the river and leaped into the woods at her left. The naked man's gaze followed them. Good. That meant he hadn't seen her!

Let's look at another example of "hanging the ornament." This one is from *The Lost Constitution*, written by *New York Times* bestselling author William Martin. He wanted to give readers a clear picture of his circa-1786 character's surroundings on the first chapter's first page. He could have taken the easy way out, which many new authors do, by having an unseen narrator set the scene. Rather, he hung that ornament like this:

Will Pike stood his ground instead. He studied the woods. He glanced up at a hawk making perfect circles in a perfect blue sky.

And for a moment, he was a boy again, daydreaming that he could see what the hawk saw: the mountains of New Hampshire and Vermont to the north; the flatlands of Connecticut and Rhode Island spreading south; the steeples of Boston, tiny on the eastern horizon; and beyond them, the sharp-etched green islands in the Gulf of Maine.

Then the hawk seemed to stop in midair. Then it swooped, pouncing in a burst of feathers and fur on some hapless field mouse working its way home.

That hawk became the real-time context for hanging the ornament of scene. Didn't you, as the reader, share that hawk's fanciful flight? It's no wonder Mr. Martin has won accolades for his writing.

I took a similar approach with the opening of *The Long Hunter*. I wanted the reader to become immediately aware of the year the story happened, the month, the weather, and the location. But how could I do that? At first, it seemed the only way was to start with an author's POV, telling this information. But then I hit upon another way, as shown here:

> *The bitter north wind strengthened this November day in 1770 as it squeezed southward between the Virginia Valley's Allegheny and Blue Ridge mountains. It had started in Pennsylvania, in land peopled by real neighbors, clapboard houses, and steepled churches, but now slipped its cold fingers through mostly untouched wilderness. It whined along the James River, and swirled around a stark log inn perched alone in a cluttered clearing.*
>
> *Young Matt McLaren stared out an inn window and watched an old man approach...*

Note that I used the wind as my context, my "hawk," bringing readers quickly from a world view to a specific time, location, and climate. The first paragraph is omniscient. But starting with the second paragraph (*Young Matt McLaren stared...*) the story is told completely from Matt's POV.

And now, one more quick example. Let's say your story includes this line: "There were torches in the yard"—closely followed by this one: "The man kicked the door in and came inside." Well, let's combine them and put the torches into the action, like this: "Torches in the yard lit up the side of the man's bearded face as he kicked the door in and came inside."

See how it works?

YOUR ASSIGNMENT

At the end of Chapter 4, I asked you to identify "author's POV" passages. Now, use your computer's highlighter function to identify author-described *objects* in your work. After the next chapter, we'll do some rewriting to include them as part of the action.

CHAPTER 6

William Brennan:
A "Christmas tree" case history

The backstory is a specific kind of information dump presented by many new writers. In it, the POV character thinks back to an event that will impact the story, thus providing information the author thinks the reader needs.

Well, perhaps that reader *does* need the information, at least some of it. But there's a much better way to provide it. Let's see how that works by converting the following backstory into action-today writing. Here are the details.

Maude Sanders, a fifty-something spinster schoolteacher in Bent Twig, Kansas, in 1872, lies in bed after a runaway buckboard broke her leg. Her best friend and neighbor Ruth Pickering has just tended to her and left, and Maude lies back thinking about her past. Her reverie goes something like this:

As Maude lay in the silence of her lonely bedroom, she wondered how she'd gotten here. Not to the bed—she certainly remembered the buckboard boring down on her—but to live fifty years without the love and companionship of a man.

Her thoughts turned to William Brennan, the handsome young foreman of a nearby ranch who had courted her more than thirty-five years ago. She'd loved him, and on lonely nights had felt his awkward arms around her. Did he ever think of her now? She'd been so sure he would always be with her. And then she went to New Orleans with her parents for the summer, and...

She dabbed an eye with the corner of her blanket, and Emma Rowley's grinning face seemed to float over her bed. Emma, who had the biggest breasts in all of Bent Twig, had thrown herself at William while she was gone. When she returned, the girl was pregnant with his child. He swore he wouldn't marry her, but by the time the snows melted the next spring they had married. Their little girl Sarah was born, and Maude taught her in school as she grew into a beautiful, happy teenage girl. When she was fifteen her family moved to Texas, and Maude had not heard of him again. She'd spent her time since, day after day after miserable day, teaching school, attending church, singing in the choir, and thinking of him.

What you just read are Maude's thoughts about Brennan. It's all back-story that plays out in her head. The only live action we have is her lying in bed. *It would be much better to mention him here only as a foreshadowing teaser, and later treat most of the information in real time.* For example, when Ruth visited her earlier, they could have this conversation:

"Oh, Maude—I heard William Brennan's back in town."

"Oh?" Maude felt a chill, and pulled her blanket closer about her. "And is he—is he all right?"

"I suppose so. They say he's only passing through."

That's dropping the first shoe. The reader knows something big will happen, but what? We'll not drop the second one until William unexpectedly visits Maude the next day. I've made up the next few paragraphs to give you an idea of how the author could drop the second shoe (and hang those ornaments) if she wished.

It's the next day, and Maude is lying in her bedroom, recovering and reading. Ruth Pickering storms through the bedroom door.

"He's here! He's here!"

Maude dropped her book to the bed. "My goodness, Ruth. Who's here?"

"It's that William Brennan! Should I tell him to leave?"

Maude sat up on her elbows, and her mind flooded with details from the past. The last time she'd really spoken to him was thirty-five years ago, when she went to his shotgun wedding with that—that Emma Rowling, whose only asset was her ownership of the biggest breasts in Bent Twig. They had a one-night stand the summer Maude had gone to New Orleans with her parents, and later she had a sweet little girl named Sarah, and he married her and they moved to Texas. Maude had loved him so, but—

Ruth jammed her fists into her sides and leaned back on her heels. "Let me send him down the road. Of all the nerve, him showing up like there was nothing to it."

"No—no, I'll see him." Maude glanced about her little nest. "Would you help me straighten the bed?"

Ruth stalked to the bed and, with almost professional movements, straightened the blankets and sheet. She puffed up the pillows and helped ease Maude to a leaning position against them. "I swear, him waltzing in like nothing happened. You sure you want to see him?"

The above paragraphs present much of the information found in that backstory, but leave a second shoe dangling. Note that they also present reader engaging conflict. Something momentous is apparently about to happen. Ruth huffs out, and soon there's a hesitant knock on the door. Brennan walks in. After some awkward how-are-you-doing talk, we may have something like this:

Maude considered his face. Thirty-five years of wrinkles had their effect, of course, but when she squinted, she could see the same boy she'd fallen in love with and still, she realized now, had feelings for. She shook her head involuntarily.

"And how—how's little Sarah?"

He grinned. "She's not little any longer. In fact, she has two teenage girls of her own. Married a panhandle rancher and is doing very well."

"I knew she'd come to something." Maude slowly fingered her soft blanket. "She was one of my favorite students. And—and Emma? She's doing well, I assume?"

He looked down. "She died of consumption. Two months ago."

Tears welled in his eyes. Maude touched his hand and he rubbed his thumb slowly over her knuckles, much as he'd done all those years before.

Let's say these two former sweethearts talk a while, and he leaves. Ruth comes in, all in a snit, but she softens when she sees the visit's effect on her best friend.

"You still love him, don't you?" Ruth frowned and patted the pillows back to their rightful shapes.

"Yes—yes, I think I do."

"How could you, Maude? After what he did to you?"

"But it wasn't his fault!"

Maude cringed at the sound of her own sharp voice and turned away from her friend. The breakup was partially her own fault, wasn't it? After all, she was spending that summer in New Orleans with her parents when Emma seduced him, and she hadn't let him know before she left that she loved him.

She turned to her friend. "He did what men do. When he learned Emma was pregnant, he beat his hand against the fence and swore to me he'd never marry her. He didn't love her, you know."

Ruth nodded. "I know. But I guess family pride won out. Marrying her was the right thing for a young man to do."

Do you see how it works? We've put ornaments from a backstory into live action without slowing that action, and we've created reader excitement in the process.

That Christmas tree looks pretty good all gussied up, doesn't it?

YOUR ASSIGNMENT

At the end of Chapter 5, I asked you to identify author-presented story objects in your writing. Now select one, consider the scene it's in, and find a way to make it part of the here-and-now action. Do the same with the others.

CHAPTER 7

Make your scenes work harder

Years ago, while my wife and I were having dinner with her parents one evening, her father said something that changed my whole approach to writing. (See the hook?)

Bill Hadley was an award-winning school superintendent, known throughout the teaching profession for his staff's high quality. On this occasion, we were discussing education in general, and I asked him how he had achieved that sterling quality.

He smiled. "Well, it's how I select my teachers. Most employers select a new staff member to fill a single job. Me? I make sure they have at least two talents I can use: the one I'm actually hiring them for, and at least one other I can use as a bonus."

I pressed him for details, and he gave the example of hiring an English teacher. All applicants may be qualified to teach English, but one or more may have additional skills. So he hires the one who also likes to direct school plays or who likes to oversee a school newspaper or yearbook. Multiply hiring for this one position by the number of teaching slots on his staff, and one can easily see that the parts definitely add up to more than the whole.

I thought about that conversation many times since that evening, and came to realize that his hiring technique could be used in many fields. It seemed to be a Universal Truth. One day, while I was writing a scene for a new novel, the power of his technique hit me. Why, scenes were just like those teachers! If writers made sure every scene did at least two things instead of one, they would have a more powerful manuscript. I applied that thinking to my writing and saw it take on a new life. I think using the same technique will make you a better writer, too.

Hard working scenes keep readers engaged

All the scenes in your manuscript provide information to the reader. That's the first talent. The second talent should be to move the story along.

Readers do need certain information so they can follow the story. Some fiction writers provide it, in part, by having two people discuss the information in an early scene. Often, this takes place in the heroine's apartment (or its equivalent). Nothing else usually—or ever—happens in the scene.

This approach is deadly. Readers sometimes feel they're forced to sit on a couch in this cramped apartment and listen as the heroine and her sidekick discuss these must-have facts, perhaps glancing at the readers occasionally to see if they are picking up what the author is trying to impart. This is another form of information dumping. A much better approach is to provide that information as part of some other action or event.

A good example is a first chapter I read not long ago about a Manhattan girl going to a Texas dude ranch. One option the author had was to sit me down on that apartment couch and feed me a scripted message about why she is going to that ranch. This author, however, found a better way. She took me right along with the girl to the airport.

The chapter opened as the three of us—myself, the heroine, and her sister—arrived at LaGuardia. We looked around, and I began enjoying the outing. I watched people hurry by, heard the throaty announcements of departing flights, and felt air gush from the air conditioners as we walked under them—the author presented all that information in a way that let me experience the trip. At the scene's end, I boarded that plane with the main character, and we searched for our seats.

It occurred to me, while I was anticipating my free peanuts and staring out the window at the tarmac activity, that the author had tricked me. While I was enjoying myself in the terminal, the main character and her sister were discussing the reasons for the trip. Sitting there in that airplane waiting to take off, I knew all those reasons, but I hadn't been forced to sit in a smoky apartment to learn them. I swear I absorbed them by some form of osmosis while accompanying my two new friends.

YOUR ASSIGNMENT

Review every scene in your first chapter. If one presents "talking heads" in a static apartment or other "blah" place, rewrite it as a scene that moves the story along as the characters discuss the things that need to be communicated to the reader.

CHAPTER 8

Don't discuss sows' ears with silken words

Some years ago, I completed a short story for a writing class assignment. I don't mind telling you, I was very proud of it. It was about an old, uneducated 1770s pioneer on a flotilla going up the Tennessee River to settle what is now Nashville, Tennessee. I recall the first sentence reading something like this:

> *The sun set in a salmon-colored sky, reflecting off the sharp mountain edges.*

Now, that was some fine writing! I could just see that salmon sky, perhaps with little silhouetted clouds lined up just so along the horizon. I'm sure I was puffed up when I gave the story to my critique partner to review. She read it over and looked up at me.

"You dummy!" she said. "This old man is from Virginia, and he's never even *seen* a salmon. He sure wouldn't know what color one was!"

I reread the passage and realized she was right. I changed that first sentence to read something like this:

> *That sun looked like a big old egg in a black-iron skillet, running down the mountainsides.*

Was that new effort great writing? Probably not. But at least it reflected the character's sensibilities, and not my own. On that day, my writing ability improved two or three notches. Since that great awakening, I've been very sensitive to language used in novels, both my own and those of my clients.

What's the big deal? Well, someone reading that short story as originally written would be aware of a third presence, along with the character and the reader. That presence is the author. While authors should stay invisible, they often unwittingly leave clues to their presence. This phenomenon is called "author intrusion," a concept I introduced earlier, and one which we'll discuss later in this book. It manifests itself in many ways. The problem is that when readers become aware of the author's presence, they are pulled out of fiction's magic spell.

Here we've cracked the door open to a tremendously important writing concept called the "fictional dream." Readers refer to that experience by saying things like, "I couldn't put the book down." The reason is that well-written fiction creates a dream state for the reader, who will on some level actually believe in the fictional world the writer has created. The characters virtually become alive, and the reader lives their experiences as the characters walk down a lane, admire a beautiful sunset, or hide from a killer. The dream is as alive and compelling as a night dream, where both wondrous and horrific things happen to us. When we awaken and remember a dream, we may smile at ourselves for having believed it, but—well, we *did* believe it when it was happening.

Every fiction writer's goal should be to create and maintain this belief in the reader's mind. There are tricks to doing so, which we'll discuss throughout this book, but an important one is to make sure the writer doesn't intrude into the story. This can happen in several ways, as we'll see.

Let me give you an example. Not long ago I was reading a client's story about an orphaned, teenaged girl who ran away from a prison-like farm to join the circus. Okay, so far, so good. In the course of events, she meets the handsome acrobat and part-time ringmaster and is stunned by his appearance. As the story explained:

She looked deep into his eyes. Why, they were beautiful. They were the blue of lapis lazuli, and...

Whoa! What was that truck that hit me? I had suspended disbelief and was really into the story, when the term "lapis lazuli" hit me square in the face. I'd heard the term before, but had to go to the dictionary to confirm that it was a blue stone mined in Afghanistan for the past twenty-five hundred years.

The point is that this little waif would have known nothing about that stone. The writer would have been much better off to say something like, "as blue as the wildflowers down by the well," or "as blue as the sky looks before a rainstorm." The author should have reflected the sensibilities of the character, not of herself.

In this last example, the character was clearly the one who was supposed to have thought the word. In the first example, the story about the old pioneer, the character didn't necessarily think about that sky. This brings up a point many writers don't consider; they should use words in the character's vocabulary for his thoughts and what he says, of course. *But they should also use words he'd use for the "glue words;" those words that hold the story together.* We want the reader to be enveloped by the character, and using his vocabulary to describe scenes is a good way of promoting that.

Here are examples of what I mean by "glue words." As our old man hikes from one point to another, we could say something like, "The path was strewn with rocks and limbs blown down in the storm the night before." That's discussing it from *our* perspective, and it's—well, antiseptic. For one thing, he wouldn't use the word "strewn." Let's say, instead, "Dodging the rocks and blown-down limbs on the trail was like walking across a plowed field at night, as he'd done many times in Virginia." That puts the description solidly in his perspective.

Instead of saying, "He lay prone on the stream bank and sipped from its soul-soothing, sparkling water," we could say something like, "He lay on the stream bank and sucked cool water from the stream, pushing away the floating twigs and rotting maple leaves that tried to choke him." He wouldn't use the word "prone," think of the water as "sparkling" or "soul-soothing," and probably wouldn't use the word "sip."

And here's another example: "The sun was so hot, perspiration flowed down his face onto his clothes." Let's change that to read: "Sweat dripped down his face onto his jerkin, which reeked with the foul odor of sour leather." He'd never think the word "perspiration." Writing like this lets us see his world from *his* perspective, not *ours*.

This means the vocabulary can change from scene to scene. When the king is your POV character, use words the king would use. But when the pauper is on stage, use simpler words to describe his personal world. While the author may want the pauper to use the king's words to fool him for some reason, he'll still *think* like a pauper, so use the pauper's glue words to show the contrast. Your novel will be the better for it.

YOUR ASSIGNMENT

Study each scene of your first chapter to determine the POV character's education and socio-economic level, and change words not in his vocabulary, as we did in the examples above.

CHAPTER 9

You say your heroine doesn't hate your hero? Too bad!

Several years ago, I picked up a self-published book that became one of the favorites on my shelves. Because of its great writing? No. Because it contains great information? No, again.

I like it because it does everything wrong. It's a poster child for all the problems you've already read about in this book and for those yet to come. The author obviously couldn't get it published commercially, so she paid good money to have it published herself. Unfortunately, every page shouts out why she should not have done that.

You need conflict!

One of the many problems in that "favoritest book of all" is the fact that there is no conflict. After I fought past the backstory and the rest of the problems, I finally got to where the hero and heroine meet. The town has flooded, and the hero is sitting atop a delivery truck. The heroine floats by and he plucks her from the raging water. I can't find the book at the moment, but I recall their conversation going something like this (maybe I exaggerate a bit, but not much):

> "Hi. My name is Jack."
> "Good to meet you. I'm Jill."
> "Are you from these parts?"
> "Well, no, I'm actually visiting my sister."
> "Terrible weather we're having, isn't it?"
> "Yes, just terrible."

Apparently, at this moment the author realized she should insert some excitement. So she introduced a young child, floating by. The characters pull him from the water and he sits on the other side of the truck top while they continue their inane conversation. Later, they climb down and go off on their adventures together—if you can call them that. I don't know what happened to the boy.

Booooring!

Readers (and editors) look for conflict in novels. That's why they buy them. While there certainly has to be attraction between the man and woman—we'll get to that in the next chapter—there also has to be fire.

There also should be conflict among the other characters. Remember the rewrite of the William Brennan backstory (Chapter 6), where we developed a see-it-now conversation between Maude and her lifelong friend Ruth? The latter stormed into Maude's bedroom all upset because William Brennan had returned after thirty-five years. That's conflict. Maude reacts by defending Brennan's actions of the earlier time. Again, conflict. Ruth is still contrary as she leaves (more conflict), and the readers are eating all this up. The promise of conflict is, to say it again, why people buy novels.

In general, when your hero and heroine meet, there should be conflict between them. Here's an example from my novel *Mystery on Firefly Knob*. Erica has traveled to her just-inherited property overlooking Tennessee's Sequatchie Valley and is anxious to sell it to fund her new antique store. When she arrives she finds a squatter there:

Erica whirled around. A tall man stood between her and the cabin, his booted feet planted slightly apart. He wore worn blue jeans and a loose-fitting plaid shirt. A leather outback hat shaded his eyes.

"Who are you?" Her stomach finally left her throat area, and her senses came back on skittery feet.

"Mike Callahan." He removed his hat to reveal curly brown hair and penetrating blue eyes. He stepped closer, and she jumped back. He stopped.

"I didn't mean to scare you."

"Well, you did!"

He returned his hat to his head. "If I'd said nothing, you'd have been even more frightened. Wouldn't you?"

She stood frozen. She should have waited for Mr. Connors! She remembered the stick in her hand and tightened her grip. "I know how to use this," she said, in a tone she hoped would sound convincing. "I played softball in high school."

Ah, we've started their relationship with an edge that continues throughout the book.

We soon learn that Mike is a scientist who is on hand to study a rare firefly found in only three places in the world, including Erica's property. Of course he's interested in keeping the site pristine, for the good of mankind. Erica, on the other hand, wants to sell it to buy a building for her business, and it happens a condo developer will soon be there to look the property over and possibly make an offer. The scene ends like this:

> *"Condos?"*
>
> *Yes, there was panic in his voice. This stranger had seemed cool and collected, but now he was hyper.*
>
> *"They'll tear this place apart. Bulldoze everything. No firefly on earth could survive. You can't allow that."*
>
> *Now he was ticking her off. Who was he to say she couldn't allow that—allow anything, for that matter? And this from a squatter, for Pete's sake!*
>
> *"If they own it, I can't stop them," she said. "If I have my way, this place will be sold within the week. And, Mr. Callahan, I will have my way!"*

This conflict heats up the reader's inquisitive juices. How's this thing going to resolve itself? Will they ever get together? We anticipate a potentially huge conflict, which is launched in that excerpt. That conflict is the "first shoe" we discussed in Chapter 1. The second shoe won't drop until the book's end.

Let's look at another example, this one from *Mystery at Magnolia Mansion*. Early in the first chapter, our interior-designer heroine stands behind a house she's contracted to renovate. She has not yet met its new owner:

> *As she eyed the van, a long Lincoln Town Car turned off Oak Street onto Jessamine and paused at the driveway. The driver, a man perhaps thirty years old, rolled down his window and stared at the work van, Brenda's beat-up car, and finally Carole's equally dented Chevy pickup. He frowned, backed up, shifted into drive, and aimed for the small space between the van and Brenda's car.*

Brenda stepped forward. "Hey, watch it!"

The Lincoln skidded to a stop an inch from scraping her car's rear bumper. The driver shifted gears and spun backwards.

"I said watch it!" Brenda tossed her notebook down and stomped over to the driveway. "That's my car you're trying to demolish!"

The stranger stared at her with owl-wide eyes. He peeled out toward the roadside beyond the drive, locked his brakes, and stepped out into the dust storm he'd created. His voice rang so loud that all of Magnolia Springs could probably hear. "And that is my driveway!"

See the conflict in this first meeting? I could have had him park across the street and introduce himself in a normal manner, but that would bore the pants off the reader. Rather, I opted to have them go at each other and create reader interest.

The conflict continues throughout the first chapter. We learn quickly that the hero wants his house repaired on the cheap. He says, "Paint, wallpaper, whatever. But for God's sakes, don't go overboard."

The hero goes inside, and the heroine considers the major renovations she'd planned. There was no way she could just repair it like he wanted, but…

But wait. What did he say? "Paint, wallpaper, whatever."

Brenda thought about that. Well, this particular project needed much more than painting or wallpapering. But it seemed to fit handily into the "whatever" section. Even if it wasn't exactly basic.

She smiled as she continued sketching. Of course she'd have to tell him about it, if for no other reason than to get paid. If she didn't tell him soon—at least before she did the work—she'd probably also get drummed out of the Interior Designers Association.

But today sure wasn't a good time.

She sketched some more and jabbed the paper with her pencil as if making a super-large period. Done! You'll be proud, David Hasbrough. You'll have the loveliest mansion in the whole county.

She ran to her car and sped off, anxious to get home and draw the new plans to scale. But that wasn't her biggest problem. No, she'd have to convince this handsome penny-pincher to cough up some big bucks, so she could do the house justice.

Suddenly, her elation deflated. That was possibly a job even the gods couldn't handle.

Again, we end the scene by dropping that big first shoe. The reader suspects these two people will be at each other throughout the book, and they will. How on earth can they resolve this basic problem? Surely, they'll eventually get together, but—but—

And the reader reads on.

Let me make a basic point. While I often use examples from romance novels, all the techniques in this book apply to *any* fiction genre. Do you write sci-fi? Fantasy? Horror? Suspense? Literary fiction? No problem! Everything in this book applies to any fiction you write.

YOUR ASSIGNMENT

Look for ways to introduce conflict into your first chapter. As an example, start with the heroine-hero first meeting, but also build conflict between other characters. Conflict sells books!

CHAPTER 10

But they have to like each other, too!

In the last chapter we talked about conflict's importance in a novel. Readers, editors, and agents demand it. If your submissions keep coming back, lack of conflict could be one reason.

But there's a flip side. Sexual tension between the heroine and hero is also important. Numerous manuscripts in all genres have been rejected because they lacked it. I personally had a novel returned by a large publisher whose editor said, "I just don't see the romance here." You can bet my next novel—which sold, by the way—was packed full of sexual tension.

What is sexual tension? It's made up of several things, including physical attraction (of course), anticipation, emotion, and even conflict. Of these, emotion is probably the most important. When you yearn for another person, you're experiencing sexual tension. This yearning is strongly emotional, and that's what makes it so powerful.

Emotions are probably subtle in your Chapter 1, and characters may try to keep them hidden. But if we are in the character's POV—and we certainly should be—we as writers want the reader to "emotionally become" the character. This emotional kinship should become stronger and stronger as we progress through the book.

Since the best way to pass information is to *show* it and not *tell* it, let's look at a passage from *Waiting for Backup!,* a novel I co-wrote. There was little sexual tension in the first draft, and I tweaked a passage here and there to heighten it.

The story involves a kick-ass female police detective who interviews a male witness who will soon be her love interest. In the first draft, their first meeting went like this:

They left the bullpen, and I turned back to the witness.

"I have some questions, Mr. Alexander. Would you come with me? To somewhere less busy?"

Notice the no-nonsense, just-the-facts-ma'am approach. Kari, the heroine, is all business. In other situations we might admire that trait, but hey—this is her intended significant other! Her attraction to him would be immediate, and we must show that. I edited the passage to read like this:

They left the bullpen, and I turned back to the witness. He was staring at me with magnetic, dark-blue eyes, and for a moment I was disoriented. To cover the awkward moment I stuck out my hand. "Kari Silvertree," I said. "Lead detective on this case." He took my hand, and his warmth seemed to flow up my arm. I jerked my hand back as if from a hot stove.

"I—I have some questions, Mr. Alexander. Would you come with me, please? To somewhere less busy?"

It's obvious that Mr. Alexander's presence has disturbed Kari greatly. She's knocked off balance, and she knows it. She's highly aware of his physical presence; she notices his magnetic, dark-blue eyes, even his body's heat. She signals to the reader that she's disoriented. Note the hesitancy in her voice when she stutters, "I—I have some questions."

We discussed in the previous chapter that there should be conflict between these characters at their first meeting (and beyond). Well, there certainly is in this case. Kari recovers and conducts a hard-hitting interview. This is, after all, a stranger, and for all she knows he's also the perpetrator. She may be even harder on him than normal to pay him back for making her feel the way she does. Attraction and conflict work well together to keep those readers off balance.

To build sexual tension, we can't just hit it once and think we've done the job. We must hit it every chance we get. For instance, we can constantly show the heroine's sexual reactions to what he says and does, as demonstrated by the following change in wording:

BEFORE: *He murmured, "Thanks" in a low, raspy whisper.*

AFTER: *He murmured, "Thanks" in a low, raspy whisper that somehow sent a chill down my spine.*

We can also use the character's imagination to build what-if scenarios:

BEFORE: *Dammit, he was invading my space. It was all I could do not to scoot my chair away or wrap my arms around myself. I was determined to call his bluff.*

AFTER: *Dammit, he was invading my space. It was all I could do not to scoot my chair away or wrap my arms around myself. But strangely, I actually enjoyed the contact. Images of sweaty, naked bodies rubbing each other flooded in, and my nipples hardened against my bra. I took a deep breath and let it out slowly, determined to call his bluff.*

Later, the bad guy has buried Kari in a shallow grave to teach her a lesson, and Morgan helps free her. The original passage read like this:

BEFORE: *I wrapped my arms hard around his neck. I smothered his face in kisses, at least I hoped they were kisses, and not just slobber. Someone said, "Dude, give her up. Get the hell out of the grave."*

Now, wait! That's all she does? She's had a traumatic experience, the guy she's fallen for saves her life, and he just gets a few pecks on his cheeks in payment? This is an ideal time to immerse the reader in all types of sexual tension. Try to involve as many of the five senses as possible, as the "after" passage below does:

AFTER: *I wrapped my arms hard around his neck and smothered his face in kisses. At least I hoped they were kisses, and not just slobber. Wren's arms encircled me, and his hot, Juicy-Fruit breath hit my neck. My lips explored his stubbled face with rapid pecks and found his lips, and his own lips enveloped my lower one with a caress. He sucked it in a way that set my heart racing. He kissed me hard, and his lips moved against my neck, creating goose bumps and a wild sensation that traveled through my body as he repeated my name, over and over again.*
   Someone said, "Dude, give her up. Get the hell out of the grave."

Note that we not once used a "character filter" such as "I felt" (i.e., I felt him kiss me hard). Rather, we said "He kissed me hard…" Tricks such as this bring readers closer to the action and make them feel what the heroine feels. We'll discuss character filters in much more detail in Part Two.

YOUR ASSIGNMENT

Be sure to use sexual tension in your heroine and hero's first meeting and whenever they get together after that. In your description, try to use all five of the character's senses: taste, touch, hearing, sight, and smell. Try also to build sexual tension between these meetings, using the thoughts one has about the other.

Coming up in Part Two...

In Part One, you put words into your manuscript's first chapter. I'm betting you made many changes and that your story is the better for it. I'm also betting you need to take some of those words out.

I'll hit this theme time and time again throughout this book: You don't make prose clearer by putting words in, you make the magic happen by taking the right words out. And that's what you'll learn to do in Part Two, which is logically labeled "Taking Words Out."

You'll apply 21 simple steps to your first chapter before moving on to the rest of your manuscript. When you're done, you'll find you've taken out perhaps 10 percent of those words. But they will be the right words. Your writing will have become sharper and clearer.

As you work through the 21 Steps, edit only the first chapter of your Work In Progress. That way you won't bog down in hours and hours of work, throw up your arms in discouragement, and go for a walk, perhaps never to come back. I'm convinced that, after you apply all the steps to your first chapter, you'll thank me again and again.

That one-chapter-only idea was brought home to me years ago by a cartoon of a sculptor standing before an untouched block of marble, his chisel and mallet poised to make the first chip. Posed beside the marble was a naked model. He took a deep breath, looked up at her, and said, "Now, smile!"

Like the sculptor, you have to tackle the big things one chip at a time. Michelangelo didn't try to do the whole Sistine Chapel at one sitting, and neither should you.

But enough of that. Turn the page and start your journey to making your collection of words into the clear prose publishers and editors crave.

PART TWO

TAKING WORDS OUT

21 Steps to fog-free writing

That manuscript you've sweated over sure looks good, doesn't it? You've reached into your soul and pulled out the Great American Novel.

Well, now we're going to throw some of those wonderful words out.

Why? Because they fog up your meaning, suck power from your story, and put agents and editors on life support. Many newer writers' work is *foggy* because they use unnecessary words that strip the vigor from their stories.

The real problem? They don't know they're foggy writers! Most will go through their lives repeating those mistakes and wondering why editors keep rejecting them. Yet many could become published, if they'd only take those unhelpful words out.

Professor William Strunk Jr., in his definitive *The Elements of Style*, put it this way:

"Vigorous writing is concise. A sentence should contain no unnecessary words, a paragraph no unnecessary sentences, for the same reason that a drawing should have no unnecessary lines and a machine no unnecessary parts. This requires not that the writer make all his sentences short, or that he avoid all detail and treat his subjects only in outline, but that every word tell."

Put another way: *The more words you eliminate without changing meaning and sacrificing detail, the clearer and more powerful your writing will be.*

And, speaking of clarity, let's be perfectly clear on this basic point. We are not taking words out simply to make the book lighter. We are not throwing them out on a whim. No, the words we want to chase away do specific, bad things to our writing. Examples? They weaken verbs. They introduce author intrusions. They form filters that separate us from the POV character. They create redundancies. They clog up our writing with misused and overused words. They allow the crippling passive voice to dull our action. *In short, they keep us from being published.*

That means one generally makes writing clearer and more powerful by taking words out, not by adding them.

This section of the book shows twenty-one writing problems that are solved simply by removing one or more words. I call solutions to these problems "Steps." When you apply these Steps to your manuscript, you'll be surprised at how much more powerful your writing becomes.

Every writer doesn't face all these problems, of course. The average unpublished writer has serious troubles with perhaps a half-dozen, and occasional entanglements with most of the rest. The question is, which ones are tripping *you* up? To find out, you need to be aware of all twenty-one problems.

How to learn the 21 Steps

Learning the Steps is actually very simple. First, I describe the problem each particular Step resolves and discuss possible solutions. In most cases, I present a *Fog Alert!* sidebar that shows even more examples of problem sentences and their solutions. Finally, I ask you to edit a set of *Exercise* sentences with pen or pencil, right in this book, and to check your work against the solutions found in the appendix.

Finally, interspersed among the 21 Steps are nine short chapters of a melodrama titled *Sarah's Perils*, which contain problems the previous Steps discussed. I ask you to edit each chapter—with pencil or pen, right in this book—and check your editing against mine in *Sarah's Perils Solutions*, also found in the appendix.

Do these Steps really work? To find out, compare the *Before and After* examples in the following sidebar. Step problems have been built into the first example. The other two—*Markup* and *Final*—show the same passage after editing. Note the Steps cut verbiage by about 30 percent. More important, of course, we've made the writing clearer, more powerful—and more editor-friendly—without losing detail. That's the whole idea!

You can start immediately to improve your own writing with these 21 Steps. As with Part One, I recommend that you edit your manuscript's first chapter only as you work through this part of the book the first time. It will help set the principles firmly in mind. Then, do the rest of the manuscript,

Step by Step. When you're through you'll have a much-improved manuscript that will appeal to editors and agents.

That's it. You are only 21 Steps away from making your writing clearer and more powerful for the rest of your life. Have fun!

A *Before and After* Example

The story segment below includes some of the editing problems discussed in this book. Following it is the marked-up version, in which some words have been struck and others added (in parentheses). In the final edited version, these deleted words and parentheses are gone. Hopefully, you'll see the big difference—often the difference between being published and not being published.

Before Editing Version

She tasted her omelet. "Why, this is delicious," she said, pleased. "Where'd you learn to cook?"

"Growing up," he answered, thoughtfully. "I was the oldest of eight kids, so when Mom died, I was the one that Dad picked to cook. If it's chickens or vegetables—we grew them all—I can cook it."

"Were you poor?" she asked, as she forked a piece of omelet and took another bite.

"Yes, we were as poor as church mice," he replied.

She eyed him secretly while they ate in silence. She knew that, these days, that handsome, good-looking figure usually dressed in expensive suits and flew off all over the place to close big deals for clients. Had he really been as poor as all that, she wondered?

"Where'd you get money for college?" she asked, curious. "How did you ever get off of that farm?"

He looked at her and broke into a smile. "I had known all my life that I would go off to college because Mom and Dad had said I would go. They were both dropouts from high school, but it was made sure that we kids got an education. My youngest sister will graduate next spring—she's the last one to graduate—thanks to our parents' vision, foresight, and scholarship money. And—well, and a beat-up row boat that played a big role."

Startled, Brenda looked up. "A row boat," she said, surprised. She waited for a few moments for him to explain what he meant by that, but he was just sitting there, a grin on his face. "A row boat," she prompted.

"Yep. A beat-up row boat," he said. "We lived in the back-waters of the White River, and every spring we got flooded out by it." He took another bite of omelet, wiped his mouth with a paper napkin that he had, and picked up his drink and swigged it. "Every morning for more than a month, we were loaded onto that little boat by Dad and he rowed us up the road with him. He'd drop us off where the road resurfaced, and then he would row back to the house for another load. The school bus would come, and we'd all pile on."

Marked-Up Edited Version

She tasted her omelet. "Why, this is delicious,~~" she said, pleased.~~ "Where'd you learn to cook?"

"Growing up,~~" he answered, thoughtfully. "~~. I was the oldest of eight kids, so when Mom died, ~~I was the one that~~ Dad picked (me) to cook. If it's chickens or vegetables—we grew them all—I can cook it."

(She took another bite.) "Were you poor?" ~~she asked, as she forked a piece of omelet and took another bite.~~

"(We sure were.")~~Yes, we were as poor as church mice." he replied.~~

She eyed him secretly while they ate in silence. ~~She knew that, these~~ (These) days, that handsome,~~ good-looking~~ figure usually dressed in expensive suits and flew off all over the place to close big deals for clients. Had he really been as poor as all that~~, she wondered?~~

"Where'd you get ~~money for~~ college (money)?"~~ she asked, curious. "~~ ~~How did~~ (How'd) you ever get off ~~of~~ that farm?"

He ~~looked at her and broke into a smile~~ (smiled). "I ~~had known~~ (knew) all my life ~~that~~ (I'd) ~~I would~~ go ~~off~~ to college because Mom and Dad ~~had~~ said I would ~~go~~. They were both ~~dropouts from~~ high school (dropouts), but ~~it was~~ (they) made sure ~~that~~ we kids got an education. My youngest sister will graduate next spring—she's the last one ~~to graduate~~—thanks to our parents' vision, ~~foresight,~~ and scholarship money. And—well, and a beat-up row boat ~~that played a big role~~."

Startled, Brenda looked up. "A row boat." ~~," she said, surprised.~~ She waited ~~for~~ a few moments ~~for him to explain what he meant by that~~, but he (just sat) ~~was just sitting~~ there, ~~a grin on his face~~ (grinning). "A row boat," she prompted.

"Yep. A beat-up row boat ~~," he said~~. We lived in the ~~backwaters of the~~ White River (backwaters), and every spring we got flooded out ~~by it~~." He took another bite of omelet, wiped his mouth with a paper napkin ~~that he had~~, and ~~picked up his drink and swigged it~~ (swigged his drink). "Every morning for more than a month, ~~we were loaded onto that little boat by~~ Dad (loaded us into that little boat) and rowed us up the road ~~with him~~. He'd drop us off where the road resurfaced and ~~then he would~~ row back ~~to the house~~ for another load. The school bus would come, and we'd all pile on."

Final Edited Version

She tasted her omelet. "Why, this is delicious. Where'd you learn to cook?"

"Growing up. I was the oldest of eight kids, so when Mom died, Dad picked me to cook. If it's chickens or vegetables—we grew them all—I can cook it."

She took another bite. "Were you poor?"

"We sure were."

She eyed him secretly while they ate in silence. These days, that handsome figure usually dressed in expensive suits and flew off all over the place to close big deals for clients. Had he really been as poor as all that?

"Where'd you get college money? How'd you ever get off that farm?"

He smiled. "I knew all my life I'd go to college because Mom and Dad said I would. They were both high school dropouts, but they made sure we kids got an education. My youngest sister will graduate next spring—she's the last one—thanks to our parent's vision and scholarship money. And—well, and a beat-up row boat."

Startled, Brenda looked up. "A row boat." She waited a few moments, but he just sat there, grinning. "A row boat," she prompted.

"Yep. A beat-up row boat. We lived in the White River backwaters, and every spring we got flooded out." He took another bite of omelet, wiped his mouth with a paper napkin, and swigged his drink. "Every morning for more than a month, Dad loaded us into that little boat and rowed us up the road. He'd drop us off where the road resurfaced and row back for another load. The school bus would come, and we'd all pile on."

Use fewer *–ing* words

Do *-ing* words hide your action? Apply this Step to chase them away and give your readers more excitement.

Consider this sentence:

> She **started walking** *toward the door.*

Do we mean she got one foot into the air and stopped? No, you say? Well, the author should have said this instead:

> She **walked** *toward the door.*

The new sentence eliminates a word. One unit of fog. More importantly, it strengthens the action. She didn't just *start* something, she actually *did* it.

Think of the readers' brains processing this information. The first verb they reach is *started.* Well, that doesn't tell them anything. Started what? Readers know something is happening, but what? The next word, *walking*, isn't a real verb, so there's no real action. The combination of the two words—*started walking*—presents a mish-mash that causes our readers' brain cells to trip for a nanosecond on their reading venture. Well, perhaps that's a bit dramatic, but you get the idea.

Another example:

> She **began pacing** *the floor.*

"Began" is a replay of "started." Change this to:

> She **paced** *the floor.*

What's the big deal? Well, *started* and *began* are the apparent action words in those two sentences, but—again—they tell the reader nothing. And w*alking* and *pacing* are not actually verbs. The combinations (*started walking, began pacing*) become mind-mush readers must plow through on their search for meaning.

There are exceptions to this general rule to change the *-ing* phrase. Starting an action is at times the important action, as in:

> *She started walking, but changed her mind.*

The planned action is terminated. The point? When you see an *-ing* verb, look for reasons not to change it. Check the context.

"To be" *-ing* phrases

We've just discussed *-ing* words prefaced by *start* and *began*. Here we consider those with a form of *to be* (is, was, etc.). Let's start with this example:

> *Patricia* **was walking** *with her head down. It would be nice if Ralph called. He'd know what to do about the train.*

We have no idea why she's concerned about the train, but we do know the first sentence should read:

> *Patricia* **walked** *with her head down.*

Making that change—replacing a weak-sister *-ing* phrase with a strong action verb—eliminates one fog unit as it adds power to the sentence.

Let's consider another example:

> *Her insides were* **churning** *with mixed emotions. Would Ralph believe her? Or would he dismiss her fears as he usually did?*

Change that first sentence to—you guessed it:

> *Her insides* **churned** *with mixed emotions.*

It's shorter and stronger. More fog is lifted.

Always be leery of *-ing* verbs, but be sure you don't change meanings. What should you do with this sentence?

> *"He* **was walking** *across the clearing when they shot him."*

This poor man didn't get across the clearing, so we shouldn't say he did.

Obviously, every *was walking* shouldn't be changed to *walked*. But the work of many fledgling writers—and some pros!—abounds with instances of *was walking* that should be changed.

The sentence's subject needn't be a person, as you'll see here:

> *The voice* **was coming** *from his right.*

You guessed it. Edit this to read:

> *The voice* **came** *from his right.*

As you edit, suspect any sentence that features an *-ing* word following a verb. They all deserve close inspection and perhaps major surgery.

Sentences starting with an *-ing* word

By now you've noticed I pick on *-ing* words that follow verbs. They deserve it. They can suck out a sentence's vitality. Other *-ing* words that deserve your attention are those that start sentences, such as this one:

> **Regretting** *her nasty tone, Betty said, "Hey, I'm sorry."*

The *-ing* word weakens the sentence. It trivializes the action. Change it to:

> *Betty* **regretted** *her nasty tone. "Hey, I'm sorry."*

That's decisive. Betty *does* something.

Here's another example:

> **Pointing** *at Gina across the campus, Ashley said, "Over there."*

Note how much more powerful the sentence is when we change it to:

> *"Over there." Ashley* **pointed** *at Gina across the campus.*

We've dropped a word. More importantly, we've changed the action from *saying* something to *doing* something. The purpose of "said" in that sentence was to identify the speaker. Don't we know Ashley's talking in the second version without saying it? Leaving the dialogue tag out clears up even more fog (more on this in a later Step).

Another example:

> **Kicking** *the horse into a gallop, the girl raced up the hill.*

Change this to:

> *The girl* **kicked** *the horse into a gallop and raced up the hill.*

Let's do one more:

> **Picking up** *a rock, she threw it at the dog.*

That sentence defies logic. How can the girl do both simultaneously, which is implied? Mustn't she pick the rock up *before* she throws it? Let's say, instead:

> *She* **picked up** *a rock and threw it at the dog.*

The following is even better, since we can assume she picked up that rock:

> *She threw a rock at the dog.*

By the way: Don't change every sentence starting with an *-ing* word. Leave an occasional one to add variety to your writing.

Step 1
FOG ALERT!

The following before-and-after editing examples use knowledge you've just gained. The number in parentheses (i.e., -1) shows the *net* number of words you are to eliminate. (Note: This Step is one of the few in which the change sometimes *adds* a word, rather than *subtracts* it.) Watch out—I've included trick sentences to keep you on your toes.

Robert came running out the door. (-1)
Robert ran out the door.

Fog began mixing with the rain. (-1)
Fog mixed with the rain.

She began jogging through the brush. (-1)
She jogged through the brush.

Bill started racing up the road. (-1)
Bill raced up the road.

Betty started talking with the man. (-1)
Betty talked with the man.

Loren began thinking about the plan. (-1)
Loren thought about the plan.

He began shaking the tree. (-1)
He shook the tree.

He started yelling, and they looked around. (-1)
He yelled, and they looked around.

He began picking up the marbles. (0)
(No change; we don't know if he picked them all up.)

It was growing larger as she watched. (-1)
It grew larger as she watched.

She was hoping they would stop. (-1)
She hoped they would stop.

Something was troubling Susan. (-1)
Something troubled Susan.

Betty was hoping they'd change the subject. (-1)
Betty hoped they'd change the subject.

She was wearing a white T-shirt. (-1)
She wore a white T-shirt.

But something was stopping her. (-1)
But something stopped her.

Would Phil be bringing the boat? (-1)
Would Phil bring the boat?

He was wearing the same clothes. (-1)
He wore the same clothes.

The pressure was making it difficult to breathe. (-1)
The pressure made it difficult to breathe.

The sound was coming from the cave. (-1)
The sound came from the cave.

Who was being responsible for the event? (-1)
Who was responsible for the event?

Leaving the inn, she went to his place. (+1)
She left the inn and went to his place.

Turning again, she drove south. (+1)
She turned again and drove south.

Seeing the truck appear, Pam hid. (+1)
Pam saw the truck appear and hid.

Retracing her steps, Jackie found the address. (+1)
Jackie retraced her steps and found the address.

Aiming carefully, she followed him in the scope. (0)
She aimed carefully and followed him in the scope.

"It's no biggie," Kim said, turning the knob. (-1)
"It's no biggie." Kim turned the knob.

"Right," George said, looking disappointed. (-1)
"Right." George looked disappointed.

Opening the door, she walked out. (+1)
She opened the door and walked out.

Grabbing a towel, she dried the little puppy. (+1)
She grabbed a towel and dried the little puppy.

YOUR ASSIGNMENT

EDIT STEP 1 PRACTICE SENTENCES in the accompanying box, then use your new knowledge to improve the first chapter of your Work In Progress. Use your words processor's universal search tool to find "ing" and decide if each instance should be changed.

Step 1 Exercises

Edit the following sentences as needed and check your work against my solutions in the appendix. The number in the parentheses after each line identifies the net number of words you're to eliminate or add:

1-1: It was growing larger as she watched. (-1)

1-2: She was hoping they would stop. (-1)

1-3: Something was troubling Susan. (-1)

1-4: Betty was hoping they'd change the subject. (-1)

1-5: She was wearing a white T-shirt. (-1)

1-6: But something was stopping her. (-1)

1-7: He was wearing the same clothes he'd worn last night. (-1)

1-8: Judy was telling her favorite story when John interrupted her. (0)

1-9: Retracing her steps, Jackie found the handkerchief. (+1)

1-10: Looking disappointed that Sarah had guessed, Georgia said, "You're right." (-1)

STEP 2

Use fewer infinitives

We're already suspicious of *-ing* words. Another pervasive verb form, called the "infinitive" (the word "to" followed by a simple verb), can also separate the reader from the real action. Let's see how to get them back together, starting with this example:

> *She* **started to walk** *toward her car.*

"Started to walk" hides the action. As I asked in the *-ing* examples, did she take one step and freeze? No, she definitely walked toward the car. We don't know if she got there, of course, but that's another matter. So let's change that sentence to:

> *She* **walked** *toward the car.*

Note that we eliminated two words and now emphasize the walking, not the starting.

What about this sentence?

> *Jim* **started to splash** *frantically.*

Jim can't swim. We infer he thrashed a hand in the water a couple times and stopped. Too much work? Did he say, "Oh, the heck with it," and drown? No, he probably thrashed until he swam to safety, was rescued, or—heaven forbid—ran out of energy. What the author *should* have said was this:

> *Jim* **splashed** *frantically.*

Two more fog units released. A stronger verb put to work.

"Began" is similar to "start." Consider this sentence.

He **began to hobble** *along the planks.*

You know the drill. He didn't just *begin* to hobble. He followed through and actually *hobbled*. More released fog, a stronger action.

What about this example?

She **decided to add** *more sugar. She did and tasted the mixture. Yes, it was better...*

We could discuss her decision to add more sugar, but do we really want to? If the decision itself is important, leave it. But the real action is adding the sugar, not deciding to add it. Why not say, instead:

She **added** *more sugar and tasted the mixture.*

After all, she must have decided to add it if she indeed added it. This change eliminates several words and strengthens the action.

What about this sentence?

She **managed to turn** *the corner.*

Should we instead say, "She *turned* the corner"? Well, maybe not. "Managed" implies she had difficulty turning that corner. It adds information. Remember, we don't want to change meaning or eliminate detail. We want to make our writing clearer.

Or this sentence?

The knife **seemed to glow** *in the sunlight.*

Didn't it really glow? That is, after all, our perception. We looked at it and saw it glow. So why not say:

The knife **glowed** *in the sunlight.*

A warning. If we say "Group A seemed to have more marbles," we can't assume it actually did. If we say "Phil started to push the button," or "Judy began to unload the wheelbarrow," we can't be sure either followed through. The lesson? Make sure of your meaning. Then structure the sentence in the most direct way possible.

Writers often use more words than needed—frequently, in the form of infinitives—to describe action. Here's a blatant example:

She's going to walk *into that room.*

Why not simply say:

She'll walk *into that room.*

That eliminates two words—units of fog—and provides the same information. Note also that one word—"going"—is a dreaded *-ing* word.

Some may say, "But that's the way people talk!" Perhaps. But dialogue isn't supposed to be an exact copy of conversations. We don't include all the "uh's," belches, and repetitive chit-chat, do we? The writer's job is to make conversations *sound* real in as few words as possible. Present the meaning without the mess.

Here's another example:

The plants **are going to die** *in the winter.*

More to the point is this:

The plants **will die** *in the winter.*

A commercial here. Nowhere do I suggest you *dilute* meaning for brevity's sake. Our purpose is to *strengthen* meaning. If two people discuss plants, information in "the plants will die this winter" travels directly to the brain. Information in "the plants are going to die in the winter" hides under a fog layer that should be chased away.

Step 2
FOG ALERT!

When phrases like those listed first below refer to ongoing action, get out your pencil. The numbers in parentheses show the net number of words to be eliminated. Edited versions appear below the suspect phrases.

She went on to remind... (-3)
She reminded...

Her plan is not going to... (-3)
Her plan won't...

How was she going to... (-2)
How could she...

She is going to... (-2)
She will...

She is going to see about making... (-3)
She'll try to make...

She is not going to... (-3)
She won't...

She was going to... (-2)
She would...

YOUR ASSIGNMENT

EDIT STEP 2 PRACTICE SENTENCES in the accompanying box, and then check your work against the *Exercise Solutions* found in the appendix.

TEST YOUR SKILLS: Accompanying this Step is Chapter 1 of a nine-chapter melodrama titled *Sarah's Perils*, which tells of a young woman's relationship with her evil-doing boyfriend. Each chapter contains sentences that reflect problems we've discussed. Chapter 1, for example, contains problems noted in Steps 1 and 2. Edit Chapter 1 by physically deleting (right in this book!) some words and inserting others with a pen or pencil, and check your work against *Sarah's Perils Solutions*, found in the appendix.

USE YOUR KNOWLEDGE: Now you're ready to apply your new Step 2 knowledge to your Work In Progress. Remember: Work only on your WIP's first chapter now, and edit the rest of your manuscript after you've worked through this book.

Have fun!

Step 2 Exercises

Edit the following sentences as needed and check your work against the *Exercise Solutions* found in the appendix. The number in the parentheses after each line identifies the net number of words you're to eliminate:

2-1:   She started to drive toward the setting sun. (-2)

2-2:   The landlord decided to increase Jackie's rent, making her bill-paying sessions real challenges. (-2)

2-3:   She watched the doorknob start to turn. (-2)

2-4:   Jane didn't seem to dwell on Susan's actions. "It's already done," she said. (-2)

2-5:   The trees whizzed by as Max started to run toward the cabin. (-2)

2-6:   "I'm going to tell you." (-2)

2-7:   "We're going to get out of here." (-2)

2-8:   "What are you going to be doing while you wait for us?" (-3)

2-9:   "I'm definitely not going to do something like that." (-2)

2-10: "Large padlocks ensured no one was going to use those stairs in either direction." (-2)

CHAPTER 1

SARAH'S PERILS

A heart-wrenching story of how one innocent young lady turns the tables on her evil-doing boyfriend.

Sarah started stalking toward the exit. Joe Howard could be so exasperating! He was walking toward her now, probably with some lame excuse for standing her up.

Catching up with her, he said, "I'm sorry. I've been having a rough day. Forgive me?"

Sure, she started to think. You just say "I'm sorry," and that makes everything all right. But she didn't say it out loud. She reached her car and was pushing the key into the ignition when he touched her shoulder.

"Please forgive me," he was saying. "Look—I'm going to leave in a day or two. Can't we part friends?"

"Do you try to ruin everybody's life that way?" she said. Immediately she wished she hadn't. She was being too hard on him, and she knew it. Her fingers started to drum on the steering wheel, making little hollow sounds. Total strangers began to hurry by on the sidewalk, oblivious to their argument. Her life was beginning to fall apart, and they were only thinking about what they were going to have for dinner. Life just wasn't fair.

Change passive voice to active voice

See this sentence?

> *She was hit by the ball.*

Note "she" isn't doing anything. Something is happening to her. Also, doesn't it read as if the hitting happened in the distant past?

We realize *all* actions in third-person POV are in the past, but in active voice we accept the action as happening right now. Passive voice seems to push the action much further back. Passive voice sentences can cripple your story and cause your readers to yawn and move to more exciting reading material.

Fortunately, the problem is easily corrected:

> *The ball hit her.*

Isn't that better? We've changed from passive to active voice. The action happens in real time, and we've dropped two sluggish words in the process. Here's another example:

> *The rain was swished away by the wipers.*

Change that to:

> *The wipers swished away the rain.*

Something now causes action, rather than passively accepts it. Ah, action! The word "by" often signals a passive sentence. To wit:

> *Is the Bar K owned by you?*

Change that to:

> *Do you own the Bar K?*

We've dropped two words. But more important, we've added clarity.

Some passive voice examples are hard to spot. Consider, for instance, this example:

> *To both sides, on almost vertical valley walls, forests of deciduous trees were peppered with darker, narrower evergreens that shot poker-straight trunks into the white-clouded blue sky.*

It's a pleasant sentence that brings forth a nice image of the valley, but it contains a passive phrase. See if you can find it, then read on.

Ready? The offending phrase is this: "forests of deciduous trees were peppered with…" Let's change that to this:

> *Darker, narrower evergreens, peppered among the forest's deciduous trees, shot poker-straight trunks into the white-clouded blue sky.*

Note: On occasion, we actually want the passive voice, either when we want to make the active object more important ("Christ was crucified by the soldiers") or when we don't know the active subject ("My car was stolen").

Step 3
FOG ALERT!

Passive sentences make passive readers. Shoot action into the following sentences by chasing away the number of extra words shown in the parentheses. The edited, active version appears below each passive sentence.

Get the horses taken care of… (-1)
Take care of the horses…

His stare was fastened to… (-2)
He stared at…

The stairs were blocked with people… (-2)
People blocked the stairs…

The valley was filled with flowers... (-2)
Flowers filled the valley...

They were restrained by ropes... (-2)
Ropes restrained them...

He has his car named for his mother. (-1)
He named his car for his mother.

YOUR ASSIGNMENT

EDIT STEP 3 PROBLEM SENTENCES in the accompanying box and check your edited sentences against the *Exercise Solutions* in the appendix.

USE YOUR KNOWLEDGE: Search for the words "was" and "were" in your Work In Progress's first chapter, and rewrite as needed to change passive sentences to active ones. Caution: Not every "was" indicates a passive phrase.

Step 3 Exercises

Edit the following sentences as needed and check your work against the *Exercise Solutions* found in the appendix. The number in the parentheses after each line identifies the net number of words you're to eliminate:

3-1:   The ball was thrown by the boy. (-2)

3-2:   Was Mary the recipient of the award? (-2)

3-3:   The game was won by Team B. (-2)

3-4:   Jackie was killed by the fall. (-2)

3-5:   The tree was felled by the lumberjack. (-2)

3-6:   The beds were made by a hotel employee. (-2)

3-7:   The team was defeated by the Tuscaloosa Raiders. (-2)

3-8:   The answer is found by dividing by pi. (-2)

3-9:   The toast was burned by the chef. (-2)

3-10:   The show was cancelled by the committee. (-2)

Avoid "expletive" and
"had _____ that" constructions

"Expletive constructions" abound in unpublished manuscripts. Unfortunately, like their passive voice cousins (see Step 3), they often rob those manuscripts of their energy.

Expletive constructions use either "There is" or "It is" or "There" and "It" with other forms of "to be" to serve as subjects (or in another role). The problem? The "There" and "It" have no specific meanings on their own. When we get rid of expletive constructions we put more action into the sentence, make its meaning clearer, and often eliminate words.

For example, in the sentence "It is important to shower every morning," the phrase "It is" doesn't refer to a specific thing, yet plays the role of a subject. When we say "It is storming," the "It is" doesn't refer to something specific.

Typically, we can make these sentences active by simply dropping the expletive construction, or by dropping the expletive construction and adding a verb or moving one out of a clause.

Let's look at an example:

There are fifteen people who have entered the contest.

Note the words *There are* actually refer to nothing. Following is a better construction:

Fifteen people have entered the contest.

Now, we've eliminated three fog words and made the information easier to absorb.

Although an expletive construction is usually easy to eliminate, in some cases we cannot remove it. In the sentence "It is going to rain tomorrow" no other subject will work, so the expletive construction must remain.

Here's an example of an expletive construction you *can* change:

> *There were good results of this test.*

Change it to:

> *The test had good results.*

Here's another example:

> *There is a good description in the newspaper.*

You can rescue it with this wording:

> *The newspaper has a good description.*

Don't use "had _____ that" constructions

A similar construction to avoid, which I call the "had _____ that" construction for lack of a better name, is represented by this sentence:

> *She had hair that flowed over her shoulders.*

Which is more important? The fact that she had hair, or that it flowed? We can assume she had hair, so there's no reason to point out that she does. We should edit this sentence to read:

> *Her hair flowed over her shoulders.*

That change eliminates two words—two fog units—and spotlights the real action.

What would you do with this sentence?

> *She threw parties that attracted the richest donors.*

"*Threw parties that*" is the giveaway. Change this to read:

> *Her parties attracted the richest donors.*

The fact that she threw something is immaterial.

Step 4
FOG ALERT!

You can blow away fog big-time by editing sentences similar to those below. Read the first of each pair, mentally edit it, then read our editing in the second sentence.

It was a crowd that was very noisy. (-3)
The crowd was very noisy.

He had a dog that kept yapping. (-3)
His dog kept yapping.

He carried a backpack that looked heavy. (-3)
His backpack looked heavy.

Can't you install a horn that sounds better? (-1)
Can't you install a better-sounding horn?

That is a color that I love. (-3)
I love that color.

He had a voice that commanded attention. (-3)
His voice commanded attention.

It was a rain that would last all day. (-3)
The rain would last all day.

YOUR ASSIGNMENT

EDIT STEP 4 PROBLEM SENTENCES in the accompanying box and check your edited sentences against the *Exercise Solutions* in the appendix.

USE YOUR KNOWLEDGE: Pull up Chapter 1 of your Work In Progress and have your computer's universal search tool find *There is* and *It is* (use its "match case" option to find capitalized words that start sentences). Rewrite to eliminate expletive constructions. Search visually for *had _____ that* examples.

Step 4 Exercises

Edit the following sentences as needed and check your work against the *Exercise Solutions* found in the appendix. The number in the parentheses after each line identifies the net number of words you're to eliminate:

4-1:   There were twelve students in the class. (-1)

4-2:   There is no one working with John. (-3)

4-3:   There were several angry people at the rally. (-2)

4-4:   There are many vacant lots that need our attention. (-3)

4-5:   The boy had a dog that was smaller than mine. (-3)

4-6:   I had a dream that Paul kissed me. (-3)

4-7:   She wore a red dress that touched the floor. (-3)

4-8:   There are many plates that are prettier. (-3)

4-9:   There were people that liked it. (-2)

4-10:   He had a horse that was wild. (-3)

Use fewer "hads" in internal dialogue

What's wrong with this sentence?

She had spent the money foolishly.

Well, nothing. It's a perfectly respectable sentence. Except…well, it's a step away in tense.

We're saying the subject had already done something at a specific time. Wouldn't it be clearer if we just said this?:

She spent the money foolishly.

There's certainly a time and place for "past perfect," which is the tense the word *had* creates in the top-most example above. It shows when one action precedes another. When we say, "I opened the can, and learned John had already emptied it," there's no question about what happened first.

However, there are times we should avoid past perfect. Viewpoint characters often rethink the past in what we call "internal dialogue." If it's only one sentence, leave it alone. But if the rehash lasts much longer, put the reader back to "that time," then talk as if it were the present. Here's a "before" example:

Hearing from Jim that morning had raised bitter memories. A half-century before, she had invited him to her parents' home, and he had said he'd come. She had washed the dishes, hung the clothes on the line, had even baked a walnut cake from Grandma Hogan's recipe. Then he had called and said he had to visit his uncle in Cleveland…

Whoa! Let's edit that passage. The *xxx*'s in the following version refer to missing "hads:"

Hearing from Jim that morning had raised bitter memories. A half-century before, she xxx invited him to her parents' home, and he xxx said he'd come. She xxx washed the dishes, hung the clothes on the line, xxx even baked a walnut cake from Grandma Hogan's recipe. Then he xxx called and said he had to visit his uncle in Cleveland..."

Note that we've dropped four "had's." Even if the word count doesn't change—it does here, but it won't in some cases—meanings become clearer. We've eliminated repetitive words and pulled the action out of the foggy past.

Step 5
FOG ALERT!

Change "had" verbs in the phrases below (which are from a flashback passage) to bring flashback thoughts as close to the present as possible.

It had been a man's voice... (-1)
It was a man's voice...

It had been close... (-1)
It was close...

The alarm had gone off... (-1)
The alarm went off...

She had been wearing... (-2)
She wore...

She hadn't been able to... (-3)
She couldn't...

She thought she had seen... (-1)
She thought she saw...

Studies had shown that... (-1)
Studies showed that...

YOUR ASSIGNMENT

EDIT STEP 5 PROBLEM SENTENCES in the accompanying box and check your edited sentences against the *Exercise Solutions* in the appendix.

TEST YOUR SKILLS: It's time to edit the second chapter of *Sarah's Perils*, the tongue-in-cheek story of a young woman's boyfriend problems. Make your corrections directly in this book with a pen or pencil, and compare your work against *Sarah's Perils Solutions* in the appendix. Remember: Each chapter also contains problems discussed in previous Steps.

USE YOUR KNOWLEDGE: Search your own writing for flashback episodes. In each one, leave the first "had" intact, but consider deleting the others.

Step 5 Exercises

Edit the following sentences as needed and check your work against the *Exercise Solutions* found in the appendix. The number in the parentheses after each line identifies the net number of words you're to eliminate. Assume the sentences are from a flashback passage.

5-1:   They had spent the night walking along the beach. She had wondered if he felt the same way she did. (-1)

5-2:   Herbert had kissed her cheek. Hadn't he known she was spoken for? (0)

5-3:   Had he suspected? She had known he was watching her. (-1)

5-4:   Hadn't he realized she was pregnant? (0)

5-5:   Surely he had come ready to fight. (-1)

5-6:   Had the tables been lined up properly? (-1)

5-7:   Had the car been parked in the right place? (-1)

5-8:   The store had been closed for the season. (-1)

5-9:   She had asked if she could have the pink one. (-1)

5-10: The box had been empty when they left. (-1)

CHAPTER 2

SARAH'S PERILS

Joe Howard had jerked the passenger door open, slid into the seat, and put a slimy hand on her arm. Well, it might as well be slimy. *He* was slimy, the way he was seeing Judy behind her back. There were good reasons to feel as she did.

"You're history," she said. "I'm going to tear up every one of your pictures. Every one of your letters will be thrown into the trash."

"You've got it wrong," he said. But that hand was taken away. Good thing, too. She was being stared at with his wide eyes.

"Are you going to get out?" She had started the car and was now shifting into drive. But he just sat there.

"God, Sarah, you're something. You don't believe everything told to you by that crazy woman, do you? She hasn't even been seen by me in a week."

She thought about what he said. She had been called by Judy from the hospital not an hour before, and said she and Joe were going to go to the dog races that night. There was something that didn't add up.

"You talked with her," she said. "Do you deny that?"

"Well, no. But I was called by her. There was a conversation about dogs. Dogs, Sarah. Like I have nothing better to do than watch them run around in a circle, chasing a fake rabbit."

STEP 6

Shorten verbs

In Step 5, we learned to use fewer "hads" in internal dialogue. Verbal shorthand also works for other verbs and tenses.

Consider this sentence:

She would be able to get her driver's license in three months.

Let's change it to read:

She could get her driver's license in three months.

We have substituted "could" for "would be able to," shortening the sentence by three words while leaving the meaning intact. That's three words our dear reader won't have to contend with.

Now, consider this even more confusing sentence:

She would have been able to graduate sooner if it weren't for Josie.

Let's make that read:

She could have graduated sooner if it weren't for Josie.

Note we've again dropped three unnecessary words.

A good plan: When a verb phrase consists of two or more words, look for ways to shorten it.

Step 6
FOG ALERT!

Terms similar to "be able to" are red flags and often demand quick editing. Eliminate them in the sentences below, and you'll decrease verbiage while you increase comprehension. Not a bad deal!

Would Jack be able to pull it off? (-3)
Could Jack pull it off?

He would have been able to put out the fire. (-3)
He could have put out the fire.

He probably would not have been able to pick it up. (-2)
He probably could not have picked it up.

Would he have been able to lift the box? (-3)
Could he have lifted the box?

Phil would certainly be able to get inside.
Phil could certainly get inside.

She would have been able to climb it. (-3)
She could have climbed it.

She will be able to graduate. (-3)
She can graduate.

Would Doris have been able to win the prize? (-3)
Could Doris have won the prize?

YOUR ASSIGNMENT

EDIT STEP 6 PROBLEM SENTENCES in the accompanying box and check your edited sentences against the *Exercise Solutions* in the appendix.

USE YOUR KNOWLEDGE: Search the first chapter of your Work In Progress for long verb phrases and shorten as appropriate. Specifically, use your word processor's search tool to find the phrase "be able to" and replace each instance and its prior word/words (could, would, etc.) with a shorter verb.

Step 6 Exercises

Edit the following sentences as needed and check your work against the *Exercise Solutions* found in the appendix. The number in the parentheses after each line identifies the net number of words you're to eliminate:

6-1:   Maxine would be able to close the shop in March. (-3)

6-2:   Janice would certainly be able to swing the deal. (-3)

6-3:   Bob would have been able to score the point. (-3)

6-4:   Tom felt he would be able to do it. (-3)

6-5:   Would he be able to climb it? (-3)

6-6:   John would be able to win the contest, hands down. (-3)

6-7:   He probably wouldn't have been able to do it on time. (-3)

6-8:   Jim had the ability to excel in sports. (-3)

6-9:   Betty had the skills to pull it off. (-3)

6-10:   Did he have the knowledge to pass the test? (-3)

Eliminate double verbs

Writers often use two equally weighted verbs in a sentence to describe actions (verbs express existence, action, or occurrence). Almost always, the first verb is dead weight.

Here's an example:

She sat and watched television all day.

Sounds innocent enough, doesn't it? Many would say that in real life. But in fiction writing, the "sat and" only adds fog. The edited version reads:

She watched television all day.

Can't we assume she sat? If she stood on one foot and watched TV all day, that would have been worth mentioning.

Another example:

Jackson put his hand around the doorknob and tried to turn it.

If not his hand, what would Jackson have used on that doorknob? Let's change the sentence to:

Jackson tried to turn the doorknob.

The new version is six words shorter and presents less mind clutter. We immediately visualize Jackson trying to turn that knob with his hand, don't we? Even though we aren't told that's what he used?

Step 7
FOG ALERT!

Writers often use double verbs unnecessarily when one action implies or is included in the other. Eliminate one verb and sharpen your writing!

She got up and went over... (-3)
She went over...

She looked at him and beamed... (-2)
She beamed at him...

She pulled him close and hugged him... (-7)
She hugged him...

She put out a hand and grabbed it... (-5)
She grabbed it...

She reached over and took it... (-3)
She took it...

She turned and looked back... (-2)
She looked back...

She went to the door and unlocked it... (-4)
She unlocked the door...

YOUR ASSIGNMENT

EDIT STEP 7 PROBLEM SENTENCES in the accompanying box and check your edited sentences against the *Exercise Solutions* listing in the appendix.

USE YOUR KNOWLEDGE: Search your own first chapter for double verbs and eliminate one in each case.

Step 7 Exercises

Edit the following sentences as needed and check your work against the *Exercise Solutions* found in the appendix. The number in the parentheses after each line identifies the net number of words you're to eliminate:

7-1:   She looked up and followed the flashlight beam. (-3)

7-2:   The stream widened and formed a pool. (-2)

7-3:   John turned and looked back at Jack. (-2)

7-4:   Someone must have come and towed it away. (-2)

7-5:   Emily reached out and grabbed his arm. (-3)

7-6:   Would you get the blanket and lay it out over there? (-3)

7-7:   Please pick up the phone and answer it. (-4)

7-8:   Let's open that cola and drink it. (-3)

7-9:   She reached over and petted the lamb. (-3)

7-10:   Would you please open the door and leave the apartment? (-4)

Eliminate double nouns, adjectives, and adverbs

In Step 7, we eliminated double verbs. We gave them their own Step rather than lump them together with double nouns, adjectives, and adverbs, because they're particularly onerous. They suck the power out of a sentence.

Yet, in their own way, so do other double parts of speech. They are usually redundant, often are clichés, and almost always dilute our otherwise hard-hitting prose. Let's look at some examples to see why we should avoid them, starting with double nouns (a noun denotes a person, place, thing, or idea):

Let's look at the organization's rules and regulations.

The phrase "rules and regulations" rolls right off the tip of our tongue, doesn't it? But when we analyze it, we realize rules and regulations are the same thing. We don't need both words.

Here's another, showing double adjectives (adjectives describe or modify another person or thing in the sentence):

That is complete and utter nonsense.

We should say either "complete nonsense" or "utter nonsense," since they mean the same thing. I could also argue we should leave both "complete" and "utter" out, since nonsense is nonsense, and there's no such thing as something being half nonsense.

One more double adjective:

That's a fair and equitable arrangement.

Don't "fair" and "equitable" mean the same thing? We should say it's a fair arrangement or an equitable one, but not both.

And here is an example of double adverbs (adverbs qualify the meaning of a verb, adjective, other adverb, clause, or sentence):

He solved the problem wholly and completely.

We should use either "wholly" or "completely," but not both. But here's a sobering observation. In many cases, we should use neither. If we say, "He solved the problem," isn't that enough?

Step 8
FOG ALERT!

Following are more examples of double parts of speech (verbs, nouns, adjectives, and adverbs) you should avoid.

any and all	new and improved
authorize and direct	new and innovative
bits and pieces	null and void
bound and determined	one and only
cease and desist	one and the same
different and distinct	order and direct
each and every	pick and choose
first and only	plain and simple
full and complete	plans and specifications
fundamental and basic	scream and yell
good and sufficient	separate and apart
hard and fast	separate and discrete
the here and now	simply and solely
hope and expect	still and all
if and only if	unless and until
many and varied	when and whether
necessary and desirable	wholly and completely

YOUR ASSIGNMENT

EDIT STEP 8 PROBLEM SENTENCES in the accompanying box and check your edited sentences against the *Exercise Solutions* in the appendix.

TEST YOUR SKILLS: It's time to edit the third chapter of *Sarah's Perils*. Make your corrections directly in this book with a pen or pencil, and compare your work against *Sarah's Perils Solutions* in the appendix. Remember: Each chapter also contains problems discussed in previous Steps.

USE YOUR KNOWLEDGE: Review your Work In Progress, and eliminate double nouns, adjectives and adverbs.

Step 8 Exercises

Edit the following sentences as needed and check your work against the *Exercise Solutions* found in the appendix. The number in the parentheses after each line identifies the net number of words you're to eliminate:

8-1:   We must keep those funds separate and distinct. (-2)

8-2:   Let's let the guests mix and mingle. (-2)

8-3:   Well, he's certainly hale and hearty. (-2)

8-4:   I honestly and truthfully believe that. (-2)

8-5:   He had various and sundry reasons. (-2)

8-6:   The reasons are many and varied. (-2)

8-7:   Let's pick up the bits and pieces. (-2)

8-8:   The plain and simple fact is that it's too big. (-2)

8-9:   Let's pick and choose among the possibilities. (-2)

8-10:   I want a full and complete accounting. (-2)

SARAH'S PERILS

Sarah wasn't sure what to think. Joe had a story that sounded honest and truthful, but—well, would she be able to believe him?

She turned and glanced at him and remembered the day they'd met on this very street. She'd been dressing a store window mannequin at Thompson's Clothing, and he had walked by outside, looking into the store's window. He had seen her and stopped—just stopped, like he'd run into a brick wall. He had waved and he had smiled.

She was embarrassed. Would she have been able to ignore him if she hadn't blundered and smiled back? She had realized that was a mistake right off. But it had been too late to do anything about it and change things.

When she had gone out for lunch, there he was, leaning against the storefront. "You're gorgeous," he had said. "Simply gorgeous. And you did a great job on that mannequin."

Flattery, it seemed, had gotten him everywhere.

Sarah shook herself from her memories and turned and pulled into the street. She was driving south, toward her apartment building. The evening sun seemed to glance off the high-rise windows into her eyes. She decided to go east to Long Street, and soon the sun was wholly and completely blocked.

"I see you've decided to forgive me," Joe said, grinning. "May I come over tonight?"

Watch for foggy phrases

I've long considered myself a good editor. After all, I spent my working life editing writing by myself and others. I must have learned something, right?

But wait!

Not long ago, I finished writing a query letter and sat back to look it over. I'm sure I smiled with pride as I read that sparkling copy. Yep. Good introduction, great thumbnail of the project I was trying to sell… I was reading the boilerplate material about my personal qualifications to write the book when—

I stopped in my tracks.

A particular sentence, which I'd used a hundred times in query letters, leaped out. It got me in a throttlehold and wouldn't let go. Here it is:

I was a trade magazine editor for twelve years…

I thought about that sentence. Something was wrong, but what? I recalled a variant I sometimes used, which is:

I was an editor of trade magazines for twelve years…

For some reason, that seemed worse. Both were crippled versions of what I *really* wanted to say. Here I was, showing off in front of editors, not realizing my proverbial fly was open. Then it dawned on me. What I *should* have said was this:

*I **edited** trade magazines for twelve years…*

Do you see the difference? The first two versions—"I *was* a trade magazine editor" and "I *was* an editor of trade magazines"—both used the noun "editor." The only action in both cases was the word "was." In the third version, I used the *verb form* of that noun—"edited"—and added real action to the sentence. That change showed I actually *did* something, not that I *was* something. Making that change eliminated two or three fog words that could put the reader's brain cells to sleep.

That was a wake-up call for me, and I hope it will be for you. The truth is, the common phrase is one of writing's biggest fog producers. Thankfully, *most foggy phrases can be reduced to a single, hard-hitting word.*

Take, for example, this sentence:

He **has the ability to** *add quickly.*

This easily converts to:

He **can** *add quickly.*

See how we've eliminated three fog words by using a strong verb instead.

Years ago, while conducting a months-long study of writing problems, I wrote down every foggy phrase I found. I soon had more than 250, and the list is still growing. Miraculously, every one I found can be replaced by one word, two at the most! I present them for you in a sidebar titled *Foggy Phrases* and ask that you study them carefully. Your writing will be the better for it.

Watch for these foggy phrase clues

You'll note that some phrases in the *Foggy Phrases* list start with one of these five words: *arrive, make, place, put,* and *take.* Your editing antennae should shoot up when you see these verbs in your manuscript, since they probably identify foggy phrases you'll want to eliminate.

Here's an example:

She **took a step** *toward him.*

Well, she didn't *take* anything, did she? That word is a stumbling block in the reader's path to understanding. Let's change the sentence to read:

She **stepped** *toward him.*

We eliminated a third of the words, and the streamlined version shows more action, doesn't it?

Try this one:

I have to **make a stop** *at the drugstore.*

That's right. Delete the words *make a* to change the sentence to:

I have to **stop** *at the drugstore.*

Leave some suspect sentences alone. This one, for example: "I want to make a change on the schedule." Our first inclination is to change that sentence read, "I want to change the schedule." However, the word "a" in the original version limits us to one change. The edited version suggests more—perhaps all—of the schedule might be changed.

It's so important to kill these foggy phrases at birth that I'm tempted to drone on and on about their evils, but I guess the list speaks for itself. Will you promise to read it over again and again, until you've almost committed it to memory? I hope that, from this moment on, you'll pause as you write every phrase to decide if a single word can replace it.

Step 9
FOG ALERT!

Many writers use foggy phrases without realizing it. Consider these brief examples:

I have intentions of sending it. (-1)
I intend to send it.

A good deal of it is fake. (-2)
Much of it is fake.

Speak in such a way that we can understand you. (-4)
Speak so we can understand you.

It has the effect of easing the pain. (-4)
It eases the pain.

It is a contribution to understanding. (-2)
It contributes to understanding.

They have a difference of opinion. (-4)
They disagree.

YOUR ASSIGNMENT

EDIT STEP 9 PROBLEM SENTENCES in the accompanying box and check your edited sentences against the *Exercise Solutions* in the appendix.

STUDY THE 250 FOGGY PHRASES in the *Foggy Phrases* list that accompanies this Step.

USE YOUR KNOWLEDGE: Search for foggy phrases in your manuscript. Use your word processor's search function to find these giveaway words: *arrive, make, place, put,* and *take.* Be suspicious of words ending in "*-ion*" or "*-tion,*" since they could be foggy-phrase giveaways.

Step 9 Exercises

Edit the following sentences as needed and check your work against the *Exercise Solutions* found in the appendix. The number in the parentheses after each line identifies the net number of words you're to eliminate:

9-1:   He gave an address to the audience. (-3)

9-2:   Joanne took a sip of her drink. (-3)

9-3:   I'm going to put a halt to that immediately. (-3)

9-4:   I'll take satisfaction in watching it. (-2)

9-5:   Come back when I've made up my mind. (-3)

9-6:   He took exception to my reasoning. (-2)

9-7:   You should take that under advisement. (-2)

9-8:   The police took him into custody. (-2)

9-9:   There is a wide range of options. (-3)

9-10:   Let's do it at this point in time. (-4)

Don't use these foggy phrases!

Editors and agents reject foggy manuscripts. Following are 250 phrases they hate, along with replacement words they love. NOTE: Search for these giveaway words: *arrive, make, place, put,* and *take.* Suspect phrases with words ending with *-ion* or *-tion.*

1. a certain measure of (some)
2. a consequence of (due to)
3. a couple of (two)
4. a dearth of (few)
5. a diversity of (assorted)
6. a lot of (many)
7. a significant proportion of (most)
8. a sizeable percentage of (many)
9. a wide range of (many)
10. an absence of (lacking)
11. an abundance of (many)
12. an additional amount of (more)
13. an adequate number of (enough)
14. an amount of (some)
15. an integral part of (part)
16. an overwhelming majority (most)
17. arrive at a compromise (compromise)
18. arrive at a conclusion (conclude)
19. arrive at a decision (decide)
20. arrive at a determination (determine)
21. arrive at a resolution (resolve)
22. arrive at a settlement (settle)
23. arrive at an agreement (agree)
24. arrive at an estimate (estimate)
25. arrive at an opinion (agree; decide)
26. arrive at an understanding (agree)
27. as per your request (as you requested)
28. at this point in time (now)
29. because of the fact that (since; because)
30. being of the opinion that (I believe)
31. by means of (through)
32. due to the fact that (since; because)

33.   during the time that (while)
34.   for the reason that (since; because)
35.   has a bearing on (bears on)
36.   has a difference of opinion (disagrees)
37.   has a preference for (prefers)
38.   has a tendency to (tends to)
39.   has an appreciation for (appreciates)
40.   has an effect on (effects)
41.   has an influence on (influences)
42.   has in his possession (has; possesses)
43.   has occasion to be (is)
44.   has the ability to (can)
45.   has the access to (can go to)
46.   has the effect of easing (eases)
47.   has to do with (concerns)
48.   have intentions of (intend to)
49.   in a few minutes (soon)
50.   in a good mood (cheerful)
51.   in a measure (partly)
52.   in a nutshell (briefly)
53.   in a timely fashion (soon)
54.   in accordance with your request (as you requested)
55.   in addition to (with)
56.   in advance (before)
57.   in advance to (before)
58.   in arrears (overdue)
59.   in association with (with)
60.   in attendance (present)
61.   in back of (behind)
62.   in behalf of (for)
63.   in big numbers (many)
64.   in certain situations (occasionally)
65.   in close proximity (near)
66.   in close proximity to (near; close; about)
67.   in combination with (with)
68.   in connection with (related to)
69.   in consideration of the fact that (since; because)
70.   in every case (invariably)

71. in height (high)
72. in length (long)
73. in light of the fact that (since; because)
74. in my own personal opinion (I believe; in my opinion)
75. in opposition to (against)
76. in pursuit (pursuing)
77. in recent history (lately)
78. in recorded history (recorded)
79. in spite of the fact that (although)
80. in such a way that (so that)
81. in sufficient number (enough)
82. in the capacity of (as)
83. in the case of (concerning)
84. in the company of (with)
85. in the course of (during)
86. in the days ahead (in time)
87. in the direction of (toward)
88. in the event that (if)
89. in the final analysis (ultimately)
90. in the foreseeable future (soon)
91. in the nature of (like)
92. in the near future (soon)
93. in the neighborhood of (near; close; about)
94. in the recent past (recently)
95. in the role of (as)
96. in the very near future (soon)
97. in thickness (thick)
98. in this day and age (now)
99. in this time and day (now; currently)
100. in this general vicinity (here)
101. in view of the fact (since; because)
102. inasmuch as (since; because)
103. is a contribution to (contributes to)
104. is a demonstration of (demonstrates)
105. is a demonstration to (demonstrates)
106. is a description of (describes)
107. is a description to (describes)
108. is a deterrent to (deters)

109. is a hindrance to (hinders)
110. is a recipient to (receives)
111. is a representation of (represents)
112. is a variant of (varies from)
113. is afraid to (fears)
114. is an illustration of (illustrates)
115. is an impediment to (impedes)
116. is an indication to (indicates)
117. is an indicator of (indicates)
118. is appreciative of (appreciates)
119. is attentive of (attends)
120. is beneficial to (benefits)
121. is characteristic of (characterizes)
122. is comparable to (compares to)
123. is complimentary to (compliments)
124. is contributory to (contributes)
125. is critical of (criticizes)
126. is dangerous to (endangers)
127. is descriptive of (describes)
128. is deserving of (deserves)
129. is destructive of (destroys)
130. is dismissive of (dismisses)
131. is disruptive of (disrupts)
132. is distrustful of (distrusts)
133. is equal to (equals)
134. is equivalent of (equals)
135. is exploitive of (exploits)
136. is favorable to (favors)
137. is harmful to (harms)
138. is illustrative of (illustrates)
139. is imitative of (imitates)
140. is in conformance to (conforms to)
141. is in contrast to (contrasts with)
142. is in control of (controls)
143. is in defiance of (defies)
144. is in excess of (exceeds)
145. is in fear of (fears)
146. is in need of (needs)

147. is in opposition to (opposes)
148. is in possession of (possesses)
149. is in support of (supports)
150. is in violation of (violates)
151. is in want of (wants)
152. is indicative of (indicates)
153. is injurious to (injures)
154. is mistrustful of (mistrusts)
155. is needful of (needs)
156. is of benefit to (benefits)
157. is of concern to (concerns)
158. is of interest to (interests)
159. is offensive to (offends)
160. is opposed to (opposes)
161. is pertinent to (pertains)
162. is proof of (proves)
163. is protective of (protects)
164. is recipient of (receives)
165. is reflective of (reflects)
166. is related to (relates to)
167. is representative of (represents)
168. is resentful of (resents)
169. is resistant to (resists)
170. is respectful of (respects)
171. is revealing of (reveals)
172. is scornful of (scorns)
173. is suggestive of (suggests)
174. is supportive of (supports)
175. is symbolic of (symbolizes)
176. is the recipient of (receives)
177. is typical of (typifies)
178. it has come to my attention that (I have learned that)
179. it is recommended that (we recommend)
180. it would be advisable to (should; ought)
181. make a distinction (distinguish)
182. make a statement (state)
183. make a statement saying (say)
184. make allowances (allow)

185. make an appearance (appear)
186. make an attempt (try)
187. make contact with (contact)
188. make conversation (talk)
189. make false statements (lie)
190. make mention of (mention)
191. make provision (provide)
192. make up my mind (decide)
193. place (or put) a burden on (burden)
194. place a credence in (believe)
195. place a premium on (treasure)
196. place a strain on (strain)
197. place a value on (value)
198. place in danger (endanger)
199. place in jeopardy (jeopardize)
200. place in peril (imperil)
201. place in restriction (restrict)
202. predicated upon the fact that (based on)
203. pursuant to your request (as you requested)
204. put a halt to (stop)
205. put an end to (stop)
206. put forward (advance)
207. put in alphabetical order (alphabetize)
208. put in an appearance (appear)
209. put into effect (effect)
210. put my finger on (identify)
211. put on an act (pretend)
212. put up with (tolerate)
213. take a look (look)
214. take a measure of (measure)
215. take a stand for (endorse)
216. take a view (view)
217. take action (act)
218. take advantage of (exploit)
219. take aim (aim)
220. take cognizance of the fact that (realize)
221. take exception to (challenge)
222. take hold of (grasp)

223. take into account (consider)
224. take into custody (arrest)
225. take offense at (resent)
226. take pity on (pity)
227. take place (occur)
228. take pleasure in (enjoy)
229. take possession of (accept)
230. take satisfaction in (enjoy)
231. take the position (contend)
232. take the view (believe)
233. take under advisement (consider)
234. that being the case (therefore)
235. the acceptance of (accepting)
236. the development of (developing)
237. the inclusion of (including)
238. the installation of (installing)
239. the maintenance of (maintaining)
240. the making of (making)
241. the processing of (processing)
242. the punishment of (punishing)
243. the testing of (testing)
244. to the extent that (as much as)
245. to the fullest extent possible (fully)
246. toward the direction of (toward)
247. two-year period (two years)
248. until such time as (until)
249. with reference to the fact that (concerning; about)
250. with regard to (concerning; about)

Remove character filters

We often learn what's happening in a story through point-of-view characters' senses. If they see, hear, feel, taste, smell or think something, so do we. If they can't sense it, we can't either. In well-written fiction, readers virtually become these characters and experience what the characters experiences. But they can't easily make that magical leap if the author has used character filters. The following examples show what character filters are and how to eliminate them.

We often read sentences like this one:

She felt the car stop.

What's wrong with it? Well, the words "she felt" act as a filter. They put the character's world one step away from ours. It's like having an interpreter tell us what's happening to a third party. It's a form of author intrusion.

Remember, we want to reside in the character's mind. If she feels something, so do we, and we shouldn't have to be told that we feel it. With that in mind, change the above sentence to:

The car stopped.

Isn't that better? Now *we* can feel the car stopping. It's not something happening to a third party that an outsider—the author—must tell us about. It's happening to *us*.

Another example:

She could see his knuckles turn white.

Change this to read:

His knuckles turned white.

We've deleted three unnecessary words—the author's intrusion—and strengthened the action.

One more:

Jane watched as he picked up a log.

See? Someone out there is explaining what Jane is doing. Well, her watching is not the important action in the sentence. His picking up the log is. Let's change the sentence to:

He picked up a log.

We know Jane is watching him because we are Jane. The story is in her viewpoint, and we're in her mind. If we become aware that he picks up that log, we can assume Jane—that is, we readers—watched him do it. Otherwise, how would she—and we—know he did it? Unless, of course, that pesky author is telling us.

Writers often tag a character's thoughts and utterances with filters, such as in this example:

She wondered what he meant by that.

Let's reword this to say:

What did he mean by that?

See the difference? The first sentence has a third party—she—wondering something. In the second sentence you, the reader (who is the character's alter ego), are doing the wondering. See how you slipped into her mind?

Another example:

He could be so exasperating, she thought.

There's that "she" person doing the thinking again. We know this because the author, who is standing between us, has interpreted her actions. Let's massage that sentence to read:

He could be so exasperating!

Isn't that better?

The above examples are good instances of interior dialogue. Skilled writers use it to bring readers into a character's mind, to let them become the character. Not only do we see what's happening outside the character—a car's stopping, someone's knuckles turning white—we also *think* for the character.

One more example:

> *I'll take the big one, he thought.*

Same problem. A third party is telling us the character is thinking something, and is using two fog words—"he thought"—to do it. We could use interior dialogue as above, of course. But let's try another form:

> *I'll take the big one.*

Italicizing thoughts makes very effective internal monologue, particularly when mixed with action. It makes the thoughts more immediate, as in:

> *I'll take the big one.* He grabbed the larger box and…

Fictional characters—and we live writers/readers—sometimes add their own filters. Take, for example, this sentence:

> *I think you're better off leaving him alone.*

Shorten it to:

> *You're better off leaving him alone.*

We've taken out two words. Our avowed aim, remember, is to remove fog words. We particularly want to shorten dialogue in order to pack the most meaning into the smallest space. Were those words foggy? Yes. We dropped "I think" and haven't changed the meaning at all. The sentence still reflects the character's opinion. The "I think" is assumed.

Let's try another:

> *I don't see why we can't dig it up.*

Change this to:

> *Why can't we dig it up?*

We've dropped three words. By putting the thought into a question, we've also heightened reader interest. The reader may well think, "Yes— why *can't* we dig it up?" If so, we have that reader right where we want her—in the palms of our hands—or rather, in the middle of our book. This is pretty heady stuff!

Step 10
FOG ALERT!

You're busy enough as an author without interpreting your characters' feelings for the reader. Write the character's dialogue and thoughts so the reader can do that job herself. The following sentences will give you practice:

He saw they'd get at least one. (-2)
They'd get at least one.

They could find the others, he believed. (-2)
They could find the others.

She wondered if the others would come. (-3)
Would the others come?

He felt the heavy weight bear down. (-2)
The heavy weight bore down.

She knew they'd never get another chance. (-2)
They'd never get another chance.

YOUR ASSIGNMENT

EDIT STEP 10 PROBLEM SENTENCES in the accompanying box and check your work against the *Exercise Solutions* in the appendix.

TEST YOUR SKILLS: Edit Chapter 4 of *Sarah's Perils* and compare your editing with *Sarah's Perils Solutions* in the appendix.

USE YOUR KNOWLEDGE: Remove character filters from your Work In Progress. Search for these words in particular: *felt, wondered, think, thought.*

Step 10 Exercises

Edit the following sentences as needed and check your work against the *Exercise Solutions* found in the appendix. The number in the parentheses after each line identifies the net number of words you're to eliminate:

10-1:   Betty felt her heart sink. (-2)

10-2:   He was trying to trick her, she thought. (-2)

10-3:   She saw that the sky was gray. (-3)

10-4:   They could see a dozen or so children playing with toys. (-2)

10-5:   I know you'll be sorry if you don't. (-2)

10-6:   I guess I'd better go check the food. (-2)

10-7:   I think he's afraid to be around when you do it. (-2)

10-8:   Jerry felt the weight press down on him. (-2)

10-9:   I think you'd be better off without him. (-2)

10-10: He was messing with her mind, she thought. (-2)

CHAPTER 4

SARAH'S PERILS

Sarah wasn't sure what to do. She looked up and glanced into the rearview mirror and pulled into the traffic. She reached to the radio, turned it on low, and hardly heard the commentator give a laxative commercial. Her seat shook as Joe reached out and pulled himself forward.

"I'm giving you a warning," she said. "If you're telling me a lie, I'll never forgive you."

"Not to worry," he said.

She gave him a look and saw his face. Her heart still did a flip-flop every time she saw those blue eyes, that square chin. He had some hair in front that curled onto his forehead, and she wanted to take it and gently push it back into place. If only—

The car ahead slowed, and she took her foot from the floor and started to apply pressure to the brake pedal. "I have to look ahead and pay attention to my driving," she said. She slowed to a stop at the corner and sat there and waited for the light to change.

That's when she saw Judy Underwood standing on the sidewalk in her stark-white nurse's uniform. Judy stepped off the curb and tapped a thick file folder on the back window. *I don't believe this*, Sarah was thinking. *No way do I believe this.*

Joe rolled the window down. "Where've you been?" Judy asked. "I've been waiting a whole hour."

Sarah felt like slinking away. Instead, she threw the car into park and slammed her door open. "That's it!" she said. She stepped on the street and got out of the car.

"You!" she screamed at Judy, while pointing to the driver's seat. "Get in. You stole my boyfriend. You might as well come and take my car, too!"

Delete -*ly* words

Back in my newbie years, I heard someplace that I should eliminate -*ly* words—adverbs that qualify our characters' utterances—from dialogue tags. I had no idea why, but that was the common advice, so I accepted it. Later, I realized my writing was sharper for having done so. But why would that be? Years later, while writing dialogue for a scene, the reason hit me. It can be explained by two words: author intrusion.

To illustrate, consider this sentence, which is indicative of many writing samples from unpublished writers:

> *"I'll advise you to stop doing that," he said, angrily.*

How do we know he said this angrily? Well, the author told us! After the character said his line, the author poked his reader's shoulder and said, "That thing the character said? It was said in an angry manner. I just wanted you to know that."

Here's a more vivid explanation. You've just taken your seat at a theatre on opening night. The lights dim and the curtain opens on two actors. The female actor steps forward and says, "John, I wish you hadn't done that."

The theatre lights go bright and the director bounds onto the stage, waving his arms. He stares at the audience. "That thing the character said? I just wanted you to know it was said in an angry manner. Do we all understand that?" Satisfied that we do, he disappears behind the curtain and the actors again take their places. John says, "Well, it wasn't my fault," and that director prances back onto the stage to tell us John was miffed, perhaps even a bit petulant.

Could you settle in and enjoy that play?

What's the solution? The way our sample dialogue is now, with those *-ly* words, the author is *telling* us how the lines were said. Let's let the characters themselves *show* us their frames of mind, perhaps like this:

> *"I'll advise you to stop doing that."*
> *His hands formed fists at his sides.*

Let's look at another way to show the character's feelings. Consider this dialogue:

> *"Don't you think we'd better stop?" she asked, anxiously.*

There's that author again, telling us how a characters thinks. What's another way to show she said her line anxiously? Well, we can alter what she says so that there's no question, and no need for the author to butt in. Perhaps like this:

> *"My God, shouldn't we stop?"*

Author intrusion is only one problem with using *-ly* words. Redundancy is another (see Step 15 for more redundancy examples). If someone said, "Now, now" to you, wouldn't you immediately classify it as a mild statement? Do we really need an outsider—the author—to tell us it was, by telling us it was said mildly? We are being told twice, and that makes it a redundancy.

The adverb adds nothing and, in fact, detracts from our story involvement. If a quote seems to need an *-ly* word, change the quote so that it doesn't. Edit the above example to: "Now, now," he said.

Here's another example:

> *"It's none of your business!" she said hotly.*

That exclamation mark says she was hot, doesn't it? Change this to:

> *"It's none of your business!" she said.*

Where possible, leave out the dialogue tag completely. This is true especially when there's a rapid-fire exchange between characters, like this:

> *"It's none of your business!"*
> *"Now, Betty, I was only asking..."*
> *"You men. You come in here and..."*

Is there any question about who said what? Or about how they said it?

Adverbs are frequently overused in non-quoted material and often are redundant. Compare this sentence:

Amy quickly jumped up.

With this one:

Amy jumped up.

The latter is stronger, don't you think? Besides, how could one jump slowly? Aha! Another form of redundancy.

One more:

She quickly jerked the hat off her head.

Compare that with:

She jerked the hat off her head.

Or, better yet:

She jerked off her hat.

More action, less fog.

Step 11
FOG ALERT!

Adverbs are used to add information, but often that information already exists. That's the case in the sentences below. Your job? Cast out those extra words and add zip to your writing.

"Wow, I did it!" George said excitedly.
"Wow, I did it!" George said.

John slowly crawled off the carpet.
John crawled off the carpet.

"Well, let's see…" he said, slowly.
"Well, let's see…" he said.

"If you don't leave, I'll shoot you," he said pointedly.
"If you don't leave, I'll shoot you," he said.

YOUR ASSIGNMENT

EDIT THE STEP 11 SENTENCES located in the accompanying *Exercises* box and check your work against the *Exercise Solutions* listing in the appendix.

USE YOUR KNOWLEDGE: Use your word processor's search function to find *-ly* words in the first chapter of your Work In Progress, especially following dialogue, and rewrite to eliminate them.

Step 11 Exercises

Edit the following sentences as needed and check your work against the *Exercise Solutions* found in the appendix. The number in the parentheses after each line identifies the net number of words you're to eliminate:

11-1:   "How good of you to come," he said solicitously. (-1)

11-2:   "Uh, we're from the Bar M ranch," Nancy explained haltingly. (-1)

11-3:   "Well, I just wanted to try it," Matt said sheepishly. (-1)

11-4:   "Hey, you know what?" George said excitedly. (-1)

11-5:   "After that, you can do what you want," she said coaxingly. (-1)

11-6:   "Get off that horse, or else!" he said angrily. (-1)

11-7:   "Why, that's the sweetest thing I've ever seen," she said approvingly. (-1)

11-8:   "Who owns that horse?" he asked, wondering. (-1)

11-9:   "I'd say there were about eleven of them," he said, estimating. (-1)

11-10: "Good lord, they're coming our way!" he said, anxiously. (-1)

Get rid of all dialogue tags except "said"

What's wrong with this sentence?

> *"I did it," John lied.*

It highlights one of the most prevalent problems fiction editors face. As was the case with the *-ly* words in Step 11, it's both an example of author's intrusion and of telling and not showing.

How is it an author's intrusion? Let's say John is talking with Margaret, and we're in her point of view. If she has no personal knowledge that John lied, who besides John does? Why, the author, of course! We readers may have earlier learned John didn't "do it" through another character's viewpoint, but that character hasn't communicated the fact to Margaret. No, it's that darned author, butting in again. Let's rewrite that sentence to:

> *"I did it," John said.*

We need to find another way to show that John lied.

Aha! Could it be that many dialogue tags—countered, mumbled, volunteered, admitted, explained, mimicked, suggested and so on—are actually the author's efforts to tell, not show? Absolutely. The author is standing by the character, serving as his interpreter. Well, we don't need him. All these words—and many, many more—can be substituted for by the one word, "said." (Some say frequent use of "said" in dialogue does not sound strange to the reader, that it's an invisible word. I disagree. More on that in the next Step.)

Authors must fight the urge to interpret for the reader. If you feel you must explain the hidden meaning of a character's utterances, reconsider the dialogue itself. Find another way to pass on the information: through another viewpoint character's senses, perhaps, or through the speaker's actions. Rework things so you don't have to explain them later.

Example? Instead of:

> *"I suggest you leave," John urged.*

Why not:

> *"I suggest you leave." John slipped his pistol from its holster.*

Much more effective, don't you think? As we did in the previous Step, we're letting John *show* his feelings.

The above dialogue tags are bad enough. These are worse:

> *"You are wrong," he frowned.*
> *"No, I'm right," she grimaced.*
> *"Sez you," he laughed.*
> *"I'll catch you," she panted.*
> *"I guess you will," he sighed.*

The point? You can't "frown" words, just as you can't grimace or laugh them. If you don't believe it, just try!

Step 12
FOG ALERT!

The following are only a few of many possible examples of inappropriate dialogue tags that should either be changed or dropped (the second line of each example is correct). The main problem? The tags are the author's way of butting in, of explaining the character's actions and deeds. Some are redundant.

> "It wasn't me," he lied.
> **"It wasn't me," he said.**

> "I don't know what I'm going to do with you," she sighed.
> **She sighed. "I don't know what I'm going to do with you."**

> "I'll charge that cannon," he volunteered.
> **"I'll charge that cannon," he said.**

"Yeah—yeah, it was me," he admitted.
"Yeah—yeah, it was me," he said.

"Why don't you go on ahead?" he suggested.
"Why don't you go on ahead?" he said (or asked).

YOUR ASSIGNMENT

EDIT THE STEP 12 *Exercise Sentences* found in the accompanying box, and check your work against the *Exercise Solutions* listing in the appendix.

TEST YOUR SKILLS: Edit Chapter 5 of *Sarah's Perils* and check your work against *Sarah's Perils Solutions* in the appendix.

USE YOUR KNOWLEDGE: Search out and destroy inappropriate dialogue tags in your Work In Progress.

Step 12 Exercises

Edit the following sentences as needed and check your work against the *Exercise Solutions* found in the appendix. Note by the zeroes in parentheses that you're to eliminate no words.

12-1:   "Let's get out of here," he urged. (0)

12-2:   "I suppose we could do it that way," he hedged. (0)

12-3:   "You must go with me!" he demanded. (0)

12-4:   "It was probably the one on the left," he guessed. (0)

12-5:   "We probably should leave," he suggested. (0)

12-6:   "That was funny," he laughed. (0)

12-7:   "Is that the right one?" he wondered. (0)

12-8:   "Leave me alone!" he shouted. (0)

12-9:   "Would you like one?" he queried. (0)

12-10: "I see you picked the right one," he observed. (0)

CHAPTER 5

SARAH'S PERILS

Sarah stalked down the street. She felt that Joe had betrayed her. She saw him running after her.

"Sarah, you don't understand," he was saying, pleadingly.

She paused, saw him stop in front of her, out of breath. "No, you're the one who doesn't seem to understand," she yelled. "I think you're the most despicable person I've ever met."

She saw a car stop behind hers and heard its horn. "I think you'd better move Judy's new car," she said, tossing the car keys at him. She saw them bounce off his chest.

"I see you don't understand," he said, plaintively.

"Understand what?" She felt her guard go up. Was this another trick, she wondered.

"Of course, you don't," he mumbled. "I didn't tell you."

She could hear more honking. She saw a half dozen cars were now stacked up behind hers.

"I think this is one of your tricks," she said.

"No, I swear." She felt him put his hands on her shoulder. "I just learned I have cancer. Judy's my doctor's nurse. That dog-racing business—she was just trying to take my mind off the cancer."

Sarah could see he was serious. "Well, I don't know," she said, thoughtfully.

"I think you should come back and ask her yourself," he said.

Now, get rid of "said"!

Several years ago, I edited my first novel to within an inch of its life. The *-ly* words? Gone. The exclaims, noteds, and suggesteds? Out of there. I made all the dialogue stand on its own and switched those no-no words for "saids," as Those Who Know advised. Two critique partners blessed the manuscript and I sent it to a publisher. A few weeks later, I learned they'd accepted it for publication.

Well, you've probably already guessed what happened. That beautiful manuscript's first chapter, lovingly edited by me and approved by my writing friends, came back all marked up. The publication editor wanted me to delete most of the "saids"!

I was surprised, to say the least. Aren't "saids" invisible? But when I learned her reasoning for the changes, I happily made them. And, when I saw their effects, a new doorway to quality writing opened up. My work took on a new life. My characters became more animated, and readers had more empathy for them.

How could that happen? Here, in a sentence, is the reason: At that editor's suggestion, *I exchanged most "saids" for action or emotion!* By doing this, I also took out blatant author's intrusions. Who's telling us the character is saying something? Why, that pushy author, that's who.

Let me make a point. I'd already eliminated *-ly* words and dialogue tags, so the dialogue stood on its own. When I was done, the sole purpose of the "saids" was to show readers who was talking. When I later switched most for action or emotion phrases—we don't want to eliminate all "saids" because an occasional one helps the work flow—I accomplished that identification while adding more excitement and feeling.

I could spend several pages contemplating my navel about this, but actual examples from that first book will show you better what I learned. Let's start with this exchange between two characters:

> "I get your drift," Brenda said. "Of course, she did sign off on everything."
> "Well," Carole said, "actually, she didn't."

The editor changed this exchange to:

> Brenda waved the rest of it off. "I get your drift. Of course, she did sign off on everything."
> Carole shifted in her seat. "Well...actually, she didn't."

Book reading and writing are action sports. See the action we added in the "after" example? We show Brenda mentally waving and Carole physically shifting in her chair. We also show something about their thinking. We're in Brenda's viewpoint and learn she is not surprised by what Carole told her. And, we know that Carole is mentally uncomfortable; her shifting in her seat shows us that.

The main point is, we got rid of two "saids" and added action and emotion. Yet there's no question who said what.

Here's another example:

> "I needed a car here to bird-dog more clients," David said.

Okay, we now know why David drove the car down from New York. We know David said that sentence because the author intruded and told us he did. But at the same time we can't *see* him saying it. What's happening while he says it? Where's the action?

Here is the edited version:

> David shrugged and sipped his water. "I needed a car here to bird-dog more clients."

See the action? David shrugs and sips. Seeing him do it is a bonus. But the real payoff is getting rid of that "said," which is, after all, an author intrusion.

Another sage piece of advice from Those Who Know is to drop the "saids" in a dialogue exchange when it's obvious who's talking (as we did in Step 12). We've all seen the results of this advice, and often it's not pretty.

We frequently see four, five, or more quotes in back-and-forth, ping-pong-like banter without "saids." Yes, we may be able to follow who is saying what, but the exchange becomes sterile. We have no idea of what action is taking place or what emotion is present. Here's an example:

> "Enough about me and the house," he said. "What's your story?"
> "There's no story here."
> "Right. Come on, 'fess up. I told you my story."

There are no "saids" there after the first sentence, but there's also no action or emotion. Following is the rewrite:

> He held up a hand. "Enough about me and the house. What's your story?"
> "There's no story here."
> He tapped his fork on her plate. "Come on, 'fess up. I told you my story."

Note in the above that we've replaced "said" with action and emotion. Don't you agree that you've learned much more than who's talking? And that you're much more involved in the story?

Step 13
FOG ALERT!

Use actions and emotions to identify dialogue sources, instead of dialogue tags such as "he said." The following are possibilities:

He bit his lip…

He blinked through his tears…

He brought his hands together…

He cleared his throat…

He crossed his arms…

He exhaled slowly…

He eyed her (over his glasses)…

He forced a smile…

He frowned…

He gazed out the window…

He giggled…

He glanced at her…

He hesitated…

He kissed her…

He laughed…

He leaned back in his chair…

He looked across the table at her…

He looked at her…

He nodded…

He nodded and reached for…

He nodded toward…

He paused…

He pointed to…

He pulled his hand back…

He punched her playfully…

He pursed his lips…

He raised an eyebrow…

He raised his hand…

He ran his hand through his hair…

He rolled his eyes…

He shook his head …

He shrugged…

He sighed…

He smiled…

He squinted…

He stared at her…

He stepped backwards…

He studied his feet…

He swallowed…

He thought about it…

He turned with a smile…

He was still frozen in place…

He went on as if he hadn't heard…

His brows knit together…

His eyebrows (lifted, shot up, raised)…

His eyes flashed…

His jaw dropped…

His voice grew softer (louder)…

His voice trailed off…

YOUR ASSIGNMENT

EDIT THE STEP 13 PROBLEM SENTENCES in the accompanying *Exercises* box and check your work against the *Exercise Solutions* listing in the appendix. Your responses will likely be different from ours, but you can see whether or not you're taking the right approach.

USE YOUR KNOWLEDGE: Search for the word "said" in your Work In Progress and substitute action or emotion for most that you find. You should be able to eliminate three out of every four "saids."

Step 13 Exercises

Edit the following sentences as needed and check your work against the *Exercise Solutions* found in the appendix. (Your "said" replacements will obviously be different from ours.)

13-1:   "Wonder what?" Mike asked finally.

13-2:   "My turn to play tour director," Mike said.

13-3:   "Well, yesterday," Mike said. "They have to have twenty-four hours' notice."

13-4:   "We'll loan you one," Jean said. "Where will you be working?"

13-5:   "Would you really sell that land to a condo developer?" he asked.

13-6:   "Oh, but you're wrong," he said. "It's every bit my business."

13-7:   "It means you need to tell me what I did wrong," Mike said.

13-8:   "Did you read the editorial?" she asked.

13-9:   "You've got to believe me," he said.

13-10: "You've picked up some weight," Mike said.

Cut the dialogue!

Not long ago, I was a guest at a writing group's critiquing session. Five members distributed pages they wanted critiqued and, one by one, read their submissions. When the third person started, I read her pages. Every piece of dialogue was at least eight to ten lines long, and some reached a full page or more. Ah, this would be easy. When it came my time to comment, I told her the dialogue was too long and offered suggestions to shorten it that would make it more powerful and acceptable to an editor.

For several seconds, no one said anything. Finally, the gentleman across the table looked up. "But that's her voice!" He turned to her. "I wouldn't change a thing." The reader looked up and shook her head. "Oh, I won't. I won't!"

I was silent the rest of the session. What I wanted to tell her was this: "You could write every other sentence upside down and say that's your voice, but editors will still reject your work." When the session broke up, I glanced at her as I walked out the door. I knew I was seeing a person who would never be published.

People love to read dialogue. It is, after all, human interaction, and we are all humans. It carries knowledge, emotion, humor—the whole gamut of what one's mind can produce.

But newer, unpublished writers often get carried away. I'd estimate that in half the chapters I've read for others, dialogue passages are at least twice as long as they should be. In some cases they become actual speeches, a way to pass on a lazy writer's research. The woman I critiqued above was at the extreme end, to be sure, but she wasn't alone.

How long should dialogue be? That's an unfair question without knowing the story and circumstances. But I'd say most passages should consist of four or fewer lines, with many just one line long. Generally, if your dialogue runs longer than that, you should either edit it or break it up into smaller chunks.

Let's look at an example:

"You know I've needed you to go through the shelves and pull out old and tattered books? Well, I've hired someone from a temp agency to help you. His name is John. He's been reshelving movies for the last fifteen minutes. I'll introduce him to you and then leave you two to get started."

I've edited that passage to read like this:

"I'd like you to pull old and tattered books from the shelves today. I've hired John, a temp agency person, to help. Come on—I'll introduce you."

I cut out half the words. But notice I haven't taken out vital information, unless you consider his reshelving movies the past few minutes vital. Mostly, I've taken out unneeded words that fog our meaning.

Some newer writers object to this editing, saying, "But that's how people talk." Ah, that's the point. We don't necessarily want to present information as people actually say it. We don't include all the "uhs," hiccups, and rambling, do we? Our sole purpose, with everything we write, is to zap information into the readers' minds without them realizing we're doing it.

Let's consider another quote:

"Okay, Jim. I'll see you the day after tomorrow. Probably late afternoon. I'm flying out here Monday morning and, with the time difference, can be in the office sometime in the afternoon. I'll see you then."

We don't need to use all those words to get across our meaning in a concise, hard-hitting way. Here's how we can shorten that dialogue:

"Okay, Jim. I'll see you the day after tomorrow. Probably late afternoon."

We've cut verbiage by two-thirds. See what we took out? The bit about the time difference does not add to the knowledge we need. And the last sentence ("I'll see you then.") is redundant to the first, where we say "I'll see you the day after tomorrow."

So, we can almost always shorten dialogue simply by applying the 21 Steps in this book. But sometimes, after we do that, the dialogue is still too long. It's time for Plan B. Consider the following dialogue:

Betty collapsed into a chair. "They haven't found any more electronic bugs," she said. "Jim has already interviewed the engineers, so they can go home soon. I've discussed everyone with him three times. There's one ray of sunshine. I had to talk fast, but I kept them from taking the sensors apart."

We can improve this dialogue by breaking it up and presenting inter-action with another character. While that will add words, it will shorten dialogue chunks while providing more reader-engaging detail and a better sense of place. Perhaps like this:

Betty collapsed into a chair. "Well, they haven't found any more elec-tronic bugs."

Phil looked up from his desk. "Good. Will they be done by mid-night?"

"Well, Jim has already interviewed the engineers, and I've dis-cussed everyone with him three times."

Phil walked to the window. The moon was just peeping over the city skyline. Betty smiled. At least the incident hadn't stopped the world on its axis.

She stood and walked to him. "One ray of sunshine, Phil. I had to talk fast, but I kept them from taking the sensors apart."

YOUR ASSIGNMENT

EDIT THE STEP 14 PROBLEM DIALOGUE in the accompanying *Exercises* box and check your work against the *Exercise Solutions* listing in the appendix.

USE YOUR KNOWLEDGE: Identify long dialogue in the first chapter of your Work In Progress and take out extra verbiage. Rewrite some dialogue to present more scene detail and interaction with other characters.

Step 14 Exercises

Following are two excessively long dialogue paragraphs. Edit each to eliminate wasted verbiage and add power and understanding. In parentheses, I've shown how many net words I chased away with my editing, but your number will probably be different.

14-1: "The urgent nature of the invitations was unusual, we know, asking you to interrupt your work, your vacation, or, in one case, a planned surgery. In the case of those who didn't respond quickly and affirmatively to our invitation, we reluctantly put a little bit of pressure on your organization. We have a 97-percent success rate for attracting attendees who were in our initial solicitation. In place of the five people who thought this was just so much hype, we have alternates in those fields joining us today." (-22)

14-2: "At first we thought that this might be a satellite that re-entered the Earth's atmosphere, but there were no signs of scorching associated with re-entry. In fact, there were no signs at all of damage caused by heat or by impact. Then we thought it might be a bomb that was inadvertently dropped, but it seemed too large and irregularly shaped to resemble a bomb or warhead." (-36)

Eliminate redundancies

A "belt and suspenders man" is a person so cautious he uses two means to accomplish something when one is sufficient. He's redundant. Well, written redundancies do the same thing. All add fog and should be eliminated.

There are several kinds of redundancies, and some are very sneaky. We've already touched on some in other Steps. Here's an example of a prevalent one:

> *"Last night" was her two-word reply.*

It's two words, all right.
Let's edit the sentence to:

> *"Last night."*

Simply that. Since it's a reply to a question, the reader already knows who is speaking.

Let's consider another type of redundancy:

> *"Why, good morning, Mary," he said in a friendly tone.*

Same question, same answer. If someone said "why, good morning," to you, wouldn't you assume he was friendly? We needn't whack the reader's shoulder and tell her it was said in a friendly tone.

Another:

> *Florence didn't respond immediately, obviously mulling over her answer.*

Well, if it's obvious she was mulling over her answer, why mention it? And who was it obvious to? Why, that author, of course. We are explaining things that don't need to be explained. Cut out those five fog units to leave:

Florence didn't immediately respond.

We could probably also leave the "immediately" out, since we can assume she responded later, and, at that point, we'd know she didn't do it immediately.

And one more:

The valley was filled with wild grass that grew everywhere.

Of course. If the valley were filled with grass, the grass grew everywhere. If it grew everywhere, the valley was filled. Change the sentence to read either:

The valley was filled with wild grass.

Or:

Wild grass grew everywhere in the valley.

A big redundancy problem one often encounters, especially in newbie writing, is use of a redundant modifier. Consider this example:

The planet was in an empty vacuum.

If it's a vacuum, of course it's empty. Or, this one:

That was the end result.

A result means the end of something, doesn't it? So in this case, simply say:

That was the result.

And one more:

Interest in writing is an essential prerequisite of this class.

If it's a prerequisite of this class, of course it is essential. So drop the word "essential" to let the sentence read:

Interest in writing is a prerequisite of this class.

Step 15
FOG ALERT!

We all use redundancies in our speech and writing. The following are outrageous examples you might be guilty of using.

A wardrobe for hanging clothes... (-3)
A wardrobe...

Do it first, before anything else... (-3)
Do it first...

He disappeared from her view... (-3)
He disappeared...

She watched intently, with rapt attention... (-3)
She watched intently...

The room was bare and empty... (-2)
The room was empty...

The untidy desk was strewn with papers... (-1)
The desk was strewn with papers...

It was completely engulfed... (-1)
It was engulfed...

Those are the basic fundamentals... (-1)
Those are the fundamentals...

Let's eliminate it altogether... (1)
Let's eliminate it...

YOUR ASSIGNMENT

READ THE ACCOMPANYING 180 EXAMPLES of commonly found redundant modifiers several times, to imbed them into your mind.

EDIT THE STEP 15 PROBLEM SENTENCES in the accompanying *Exercise* box and check your work against the *Exercise Solutions* listing in the appendix.

TEST YOUR SKILLS: Edit Chapter 6 of *Sarah's Perils* and check your work against *Sarah's Perils Solutions* in the appendix.

USE YOUR KNOWLEDGE: Search out and destroy redundancies in your Work In Progress.

180 Redundant Modifiers

a ~~dollar amount of~~ $500
add ~~more~~ resources
~~alternative~~ choice
an accountant ~~by occupation~~
an innovative ~~new~~ concept
analyze ~~in depth~~
~~anecdotal~~ story
audible ~~to the ear~~
~~authentic~~ replica
~~basic~~ essentials
~~basic~~ fundamental
biography ~~of her life~~
~~brand~~ new
changes ~~and alterations~~
circulate ~~around~~
classify ~~into groups~~
~~close~~ proximity
~~close~~ scrutiny
~~complete~~ monopoly
~~complete~~ stop
~~completely~~ destroyed
~~completely~~ engulfed
~~completely~~ unanimous
~~component~~ part

consensus ~~of opinion~~
~~continent of~~ Africa
continue ~~on~~
~~contract~~ agreement
cooperate ~~together~~
costs ~~and expenses~~
could ~~possibly~~
~~daily~~ per diem
~~dead~~ body
decapitate ~~his head~~
~~deliberate~~ arson
disappear ~~from sight~~
~~duplicate~~ copy
dwindle ~~down~~
each ~~and every~~
~~early~~ beginnings
eliminate ~~altogether~~
~~empty~~ vacuum
~~end~~ result
~~essential~~ prerequisite
~~established~~ standard
~~established~~ tradition
every ~~single~~
evolve ~~over time~~

exactly the same

final conclusion

final outcome

firm commitment

firm conviction

first and foremost

first created

first introduced

first invented

focus in

follow after

forecast future events

foretell future sales

free complementary coffee

free gift

full and complete stop

full to capacity

fundamental basis

future plans

future projections

future to come

general consensus

global demand around the world

go abroad to other countries

go down into a decline

have in my possession

hollow tube

honest truth

huddle together

huge throng

illustrative example

important essentials

improve and enhance

insignificant and unimportant

intentional fraud

invited guest

joint agreement

joint cooperation

kill dead

lag behind

large/small in size

last of all

listen in

little child

long litany

look forward into the future

loudly bellow

mass exodus

mass extinction

match exactly

mental telepathy

merge together

more improved

more inferior

more preferable

more superior

most favorite

most, but not all

mutual agreement

necessary essential

necessary prerequisite

necessary requirement

never at any time

new innovation

not one single animal

original creator

original founder

pair in twos

pair of twins

past achievement

past experience

past history

period of three hours

personal friend

personal opinion

~~personal~~ rapport
pick ~~and choose~~
plan ~~ahead~~
plan ~~in advance~~
~~popular~~ consensus
postpone ~~until later~~
~~preliminary~~ draft
prepay ~~first~~
~~proven~~ fact
~~qualified~~ expert
~~quickly~~ expedite
~~ratio of~~ two to one
~~rational~~ reason
reason ~~why~~
recite ~~back~~
~~regular~~ routine
reiterate ~~again~~
relate ~~back~~
repeat ~~again~~
report ~~back~~
resume ~~again~~
retreat ~~back~~
return ~~back~~
reuse ~~again~~
revert ~~back~~
~~safe~~ haven
~~same~~ identical
scrutinize ~~in detail~~
seesaw ~~up and down~~
separate ~~apart~~
~~short~~ summary
shorter/longer ~~in length~~
skirt ~~around~~
~~slight~~ trace
spliced ~~together~~
square ~~in shape~~
~~sum~~ total
summarize ~~briefly~~

surround ~~on all sides~~
~~sworn~~ affidavit
~~temporary~~ interim director
~~temporary~~ stopgap
~~terrible~~ tragedy
think ~~to myself~~
tiny ~~little~~
together ~~as a team~~
~~total of~~ ten people
~~true~~ fact
two ~~twins~~
~~usual~~ custom
vacillate ~~back and forth~~
~~violent~~ explosion
~~vital~~ necessity
white ~~albino~~
~~white~~ snow
~~whole~~ repertoire
widow ~~woman~~

Step 15 Exercises

Edit the following sentences as needed and check your work against the *Exercise Solutions* found in the appendix.

15-1:   "You sure?" He seemed a little uncertain. (-5)

15-2:   "John!" Sarah looked at him in alarm. (-2)

15-3:   "Who cares?" Bob waved that problem aside. (-5)

15-4:   "Are you back on that Phil kick again?" Sarah asked, her tone hostile. (-3)

15-5:   "I didn't know it was a sensitive issue," Kermit said, as if in surrender. (-4)

15-6:   "This is an authentic replica." (-1)

15-7:   "I'm convinced it was deliberate arson." (-1)

15-8:   "I think we should cooperate together." (-1)

15-9:   "I have three of those in my possession." (-3)

15-10: "This is an improved and enhanced model." (-2)

CHAPTER 6

SARAH'S PERILS

Sarah stared at Joe. "I don't know whether to believe you or not," she said, a touch of doubt in her voice. "A part of me wants to, but some things don't seem to add up. Am I to really believe you have cancer? It would seem to me that you would have told me about that sooner, and not wait until now. Why, if you really do have it, that's awful. I—"

"Why shouldn't you believe me," he said, questioningly. "Look—I'm dying of cancer. Why would I want to lie?"

"Well, I don't believe it," she said, thinking he was probably lying.

He took her hand. "Come ask Judy," he said in a pleading way. "She'll tell you."

"I—I guess it couldn't hurt," she said hesitantly. She started following him to her car. Judy, standing by the door, appeared nervous.

"I told her about my cancer," Joe said loudly. "You know—the cancer you came to tell me about?"

Judy stared blankly at him for several seconds, obviously thinking about what he said. "The—the cancer?" she said, after a pause.

"The cancer you came to tell me about, remember?" he said, almost repeating himself. "I told Sarah you were just giving me more information about it."

"Oh, *that* cancer!" Judy said, reaching out and touching Sarah's arm. "That's what the doctor said."

"Oh, goodness," Sarah started to say. "Joe, I'm so sorry."

Wait. Something was amiss. Something about Judy's hand...

"Is something wrong?" Joe asked.

That—that ring on Judy's hand! "Oh, I see it all now," she said, as if she realized something. "Joe—that's your ring!"

Use fewer prepositional phrases

"Of the," "by the," "on the," "to the," "in the," and similar phrase-starters often add fog. The first words—by, on, to, etc.—are called prepositions, and they link nouns, pronouns, and phrases to other words in a sentence.

An example:

He pulled large rocks away from the mouth of the cave.

The cave is the important idea, but we've made the "mouth" the sentence's focus. The readers see "mouth" first, not "cave," and might trip for a nanosecond before reading the word "cave." Let's solve that problem by changing the sentence to read:

He pulled large rocks away from the cave's mouth.

Not a big deal? Well, it certainly can be. The second version is clearer and shorter. Making similar changes throughout your manuscript will decrease verbiage and increase readability.

Often, we can throw away an "of the" without using an apostrophe. Here's an example:

That's one of the reasons his pack weighs so much.

Change that to:

That's one reason his pack weighs so much.

Here's another example:

She spread a blanket on the grassy bank of the river.

Let's change that to:

She spread a blanket on the grassy riverbank.

We've taken out two fog words, changed the sentence's object, and made the sentence easier for the reader to absorb.

Here's another problem sentence:

He grabbed the handle of the door, which had been bashed in.

We might contract the sentence this way:

He grabbed the door's handle, which had been bashed in.

But there's a problem with this rewrite. Do you see it? The revised sentence implies the handle, not the door, was the thing bashed in. Let's change it to:

He grabbed the bashed-in door's handle.

Some phrases should be left alone simply because they sound better the way they are. For example:

When they got to the bottom of the stairs...

sounds better than

When they got to the stairs' bottom...

But leave-it-alone examples aren't nearly as prevalent as change-it examples.

Consider this one:

The walls of the room were blue.

This becomes:

The room's walls were blue.

And one more:

Joan slapped her on the face.

Let's change that to:

Joan slapped her face.

We can often eliminate phrases completely. To illustrate, we'll transform sentences through two editing stages:

The door to the room was open.
The room's door was open.
The door was open.

The floor in the barn was wet.
The barn floor was wet.
The floor was wet.

The seats in the car were torn.
The car seats were torn.
The seats were torn.

In each case, if a non-point-of-view character is explaining what she saw to another character, the second version is correct. But if a point-of-view character sees the object (the door, floor, or seats) she (and we) know its location, and we can eliminate the modifier.

Look how many fog words we've chased away!

Step 16
FOG ALERT!

Prepositional phrases provide information, but often at the expense of clarity. Here are fast phrase fixes.

Wall along the staircase... (-2)
Staircase wall...

Room at the hotel... (-2)
Hotel room...

He took her by the hand... (-2)
He took her hand...

Best place for pizza... (-1)
Best pizza place...

Artist from the 1890s... (-2)
1890s artist...

Muscles in his legs... (-1)
His leg muscles...

Anger in his voice... (-2)
Angry voice...

Edge of the table... (-2)
Table edge...

Side of the road... (-3)
Roadside...

Light of the sun... (-3)
Sunlight...

Fragments of glass... (-1)
Glass fragments...

Shutters on the window... (-2)
Window shutters...

Hit him on the shoulder... (-2)
Hit his shoulder...

YOUR ASSIGNMENT

EDIT THE STEP 16 PROBLEM SENTENCES in the *Exercise* box and check your work against the *Exercise Solutions* listing in the appendix.

USE YOUR KNOWLEDGE: Use your computer's search function to find phrase-starters "of the," "by the," "on the," "to the," and "in the" in your Work In Progress and rework those sentences to bring the object word to the forefront.

Step 16 Exercises

Edit the following sentences as needed and check your work against the *Exercise Solutions* found in the appendix. The number in the parentheses after each line identifies the net number of words you're to eliminate:

16-1:   The rain pummeled the roof of the car. (-2)

16-2:   A window in the bedroom had been raised a few inches. (-2)

16-3:   They wandered through the streets of the town. (-2)

16-4:   Bill lounged against the hood of the car. (-2)

16-5:   She marched to the open passenger door of the van. (-2)

16-6:   He was a doctor from the country. (-2)

16-7:   Please give me the contents of that drawer. (-2)

16-8:   It was the last skit of the show. (-2)

16-9:   It was the largest one in the group. (-2)

16-10: It leaned against the north wall of the house. (-2)

Get rid of throwaway words

We frequently use extra words and phrases without thinking. They sound and look right, so we think they must be right. But these extra words are extra, nonetheless. They add fog, and fog chases readers away. So let's target these unneeded words.

Consider, for example, this sentence:

Ahead of them was a muddy, rutted road.

Well, who else could it be ahead of, if not them? Take "of them" out to make the sentence read:

Ahead was a muddy, rutted road.

Here's another:

The women brought the children toys to play with.

Think about it: What else would the children do with the toys if not play with them? We should obviously change this sentence to read:

The women brought the children toys.

Perhaps the most egregious example of an overused word is *that*. I recently removed more than eight hundred *that*s from a novel, making the copy much easier to read. Here's a common example:

I think that I'll take it.

Change the sentence to read:

I think I'll take it.

You'll probably find many unnecessary *that*s in your Work In Progress. We use the word for many purposes: an adjective (*that* string is broken), a pronoun (after *that*, she shut up), an adverb (is it *that* bad?), and a conjunction. It's this last use—where *that* introduces a clause—that's foggy.

Here's an example:

> She knew **that** *Jack was going to meet June.*

What would happen if we took the *that* out? Well, the sentence would become clearer:

> *She knew Jack was going to meet June.*

Then is another overused word. It's used as a noun (until *then*, I'll stay), an adjective (Harding, the *then* president), and in several ways as an adverb. The latter—to show time, space, or order—is overused in writing.

Some unedited manuscripts are peppered with *then*s, making them sound like kindergarten children's recital of what they did last summer:

> *"We went to Disney World,* **then** *we visited 'It's a Small World,'* **then** *we…"*

In many cases, the word *then* is not needed, since we usually tell stories in chronological order and the *then* is assumed.

Consider its use in this sentence:

> **Then** *her face clouded over.*

Something caused that girl's face to cloud over. Her boyfriend broke up with her, she had a sad thought—something happened first and we, the reader, often know what it was. Since that's true, why can't we edit the line to read: "Her face clouded over." Well, we can!

Suddenly is another overused word. Consider, for example, this sentence:

> **Suddenly** *the trail ended in a clearing.*

How else can that trail end, if not suddenly? Slowly? Of course the trail's end was sudden. So why mention it? The author really meant the viewpoint character saw the clearing ahead. So, why not just say:

> *The trail ended in a clearing.*

Or, perhaps:

A clearing appeared ahead.

Suddenly implies something happens fast, without warning. But often the sentence already says that (if it doesn't, rewrite it so it does). It's another belt-and-suspenders case. For example:

*She **suddenly** hiccupped.*

Aren't all hiccups sudden? Have you ever planned one? Change that line to:

She hiccupped.

Doesn't that tell the story?

Just is another throwaway word. It is used both as an adjective (*just desserts, just ruler, just appraisal*) and as an adverb. It's the latter use that sometimes gives us problems.

There's often no need to use the word *just*. Consider a fictional character who saw a friend running and called out to her to stop, but she doesn't. He tells us:

*She **just** kept running.*

Do we need that *just*? It implies the friend is ignoring the command. But doesn't the sentence do that without the word?

How about this sentence?

*She was **just** about ready to do it.*

Let's leave the word *just* out, to leave this:

She was about ready to do it.

Doesn't that say the same thing? What meaning does *just* add?

The list of throwaway words is long. Common examples include *up, down, out, off, over,* and *very.* We've highlighted some in the *Fog Alert!* below, and noted others in the Step 17 *Exercises.* We've also included a list of more than a hundred examples in the accompanying box labeled *Extra Words.*

Step 17
FOG ALERT!

Learn to scrutinize your writing in order to avoid including those pesky "extra words." The following wordy sentences are examples.

He'll come in the month of December.
He'll come in December.

The field of science is complex.
Science is complex.

Bring the apples last of all.
Bring the apples last.

The flowers are located in the church.
The flowers are in the church.

He dragged the logs up to the woodpile.
He dragged the logs to the woodpile.

Bill stood up and addressed the crowd.
Bill stood and addressed the crowd.

He looked down at the ground.
He looked at the ground.

She slowed down and looked out the windshield.
She slowed and looked out the windshield.

She sat down on the bed.
She sat on the bed.

He peered out from under the rug.
He peered from under the rug.

Water flowed out into the road.
Water flowed into the road.

He helped out with the planning.
He helped with the planning.

He stuffed some tobacco into his pipe.
He stuffed tobacco into his pipe.

We need some help.
We need help.

YOUR ASSIGNMENT

EDIT THE STEP 17 PROBLEM SENTENCES in the accompanying *Exercise* box and check your work against the *Exercise Solutions* in the appendix.

TEST YOUR SKILLS: Edit Chapter 7 of *Sarah's Perils* and check your work against *Sarah's Perils Solutions* in the appendix.

STUDY THE ACCOMPANYING LIST titled *Throwaway Words*. You're sure to find several no-no words that habitually creep into your writing.

USE YOUR KNOWLEDGE: Search out and destroy throwaway words in the first chapter of your Work In Progress. Use your word processor's search tool to locate these specific ones: *that, then, up, down, out, off, over, suddenly, just, some,* and *very*.

Step 17 Exercises

Edit the following sentences as needed and check your work against the *Exercise Solutions* listing found in the appendix. The number in the parentheses after each line identifies the net number of words you're to eliminate:

17-1:   They heard the noise of children in the playground. (-3)

17-2:   Debris blocked off the path. (-1)

17-3:   He walked over to the window. (-1)

17-4:   "We're wondering which trails we want to take." (-2)

17-5:   Each of them wondered what would happen. (-2)

17-6:   Ahead of her, a stocky boy sat on the diving board. (-2)

17-7:   But her thoughts were a million miles away at that moment. (-3)

17-8:   The sky above was cloudy. (-1)

17-9:   He wants to try to understand the problem. (-2)

17-10: He disappeared from sight. (-2)

SARAH'S PERILS

Anger warmed the cheeks of Sarah's face. She put the palm of her hand on the door, which was open, for support.

Joe said, "Well, what really happened was—"

She slid into the driver's seat. "Forget it, Joe. You two get away from my car!"

Judy moved away from the car and stepped onto the edge of the sidewalk, and Joe slammed the door of the car closed. "You don't know what you're doing," he said. "The doctor said I have cancer of the lungs."

"Right." Sarah had a head that throbbed, and a boyfriend who was being unfaithful. Which was worse?

Sarah slammed the gearshift home and screeched out. She turned left at the next corner of the street, swerving to miss traffic coming her way. That Joe was going to get his, she fumed. He—

Her cell phone rang, and she jumped. She opened it and spoke into the mouthpiece. "Hello?"

"It's me." Joe's voice. "Don't hang up! Can I trust you?"

"What?"

"I need to talk with you about something of importance to the nation. It has to do with the CIA. I'll be at your place at eight this evening. Be there."

He hung up, ending the conversation.

Throwaway Words

Extra words abound in writing, particularly in the work of new writers. Following are more than 100 examples of throwaway words that should be edited out of your Work In Progress.

a ~~matter of~~ concern	hurry ~~up~~
~~active~~ role	idea is big ~~in scope~~
~~actual~~ experience	~~job of~~ frying the eggs
add ~~up~~	~~kind of~~ wandered into it
advance ~~up~~	listen ~~in~~
all day ~~long~~	~~located~~ at the church
~~all-time~~ record	lose ~~out on~~
balance ~~out~~	made ~~a~~ long ~~time~~ ago
~~based~~ in Chicago, IL	~~man who is~~ strong (man)
beginning ~~point~~	match ~~up~~
block ~~out~~	mix ~~together~~
blue ~~in color~~	open ~~up~~
botch ~~up~~	~~or anything~~
~~by their nature~~	~~or something~~
close ~~down~~	~~or whatever~~
close ~~up~~	phone ~~up~~
cloth ~~made of~~ cotton (cloth)	polish ~~up~~
divide ~~up~~	rise ~~up~~
easiest ~~of all~~	seal ~~up~~
~~exists to~~ support	seek ~~out~~
fall ~~down~~	~~sense of~~ foreboding
find ~~out~~	serve ~~up~~
finish ~~up~~	shake ~~up~~
first ~~of all~~	shut ~~down~~
fold ~~up~~	~~six-legged~~ insect
~~for your information~~	stall ~~for time~~
free ~~up~~	start ~~off~~
has ~~got~~	start ~~out~~
have ~~in fact~~ changed	storm ~~activity~~
head ~~up~~	study ~~up~~
heat ~~up~~	sum ~~up~~
help ~~out~~	switch ~~over~~
~~hot~~ water heater	tense ~~up~~

test ~~out~~
~~the area of~~ math
~~the existence of~~
~~the extent of~~ funding
~~the feeling of~~ remorse
~~the field of~~ science
~~the function of~~ refereeing
~~the idea of~~ selling short
~~the issue of~~ marching
~~the medium of~~
~~the method of~~
~~the notion of~~
~~the practice of~~
~~the presence of~~
~~the principal of~~
~~the procedures of~~
~~the process of~~
~~the purpose of~~
~~the question of~~
~~the reality of~~
~~the realm of~~
~~the region of~~
~~the role of~~
~~the scale of~~
~~the scope of~~
~~the space of~~
~~the state of~~
the ~~whole~~ project
they are different ~~in nature~~
~~to the tune of~~
total ~~up~~
~~traveling~~ northbound
tuna ~~fish~~
~~very~~ end
~~very~~ saturated
~~very~~ unique
wrinkled ~~in appearance~~
your ~~particular~~ area

Edit for conciseness

In Step 9, we watched for foggy phrases. Here, we both combine and condense phrases, but these aren't predictable phrases like the ones from the earlier chapter. They are unique ones with extra verbiage that creeps into our writing almost by osmosis and seem to belong there. They do not!

We must develop a sixth sense to root out that extra verbiage. As you edit your work, constantly ask yourself if there isn't a shorter way to write each sentence. You'll soon be editing both yourself and the authors of schlock books we all seem to find on the bookstands.

Let's look at examples of this particular fog:

> *The rain continued to come down harder and harder.*

Let's say, instead:

> *It rained harder and harder.*

The deleted phrase—five foggy words long—is mind garbage. Another example:

> *Penny tried to scream, but the sound caught in her throat.*

Change that to:

> *Penny's scream caught in her throat.*

We've dropped half the words! We've traded a mish-mash for a sharp wham-bam sentence that grabs the reader. We realize that, if Penny's scream caught in her throat, she must have tried to scream.

Look also for ways to cut verbiage by combining sentences. Here's an example we sometimes see in amateur writing:

> *The ball was blue. It bounced down the road.*

This becomes:

> *The blue ball bounced down the road.*

Most potential sentence combinations, of course, aren't that obvious. Here's an example:

> *Patrons sat at the computers, tapping at the keyboards. Most were kids doing their homework.*

That can easily be changed to:

> *Patrons, mostly kids doing their homework, tapped on computer keyboards.*

Examples of superfluous verbiage abound in the work of unpublished writers. To prove the point—and hopefully provide good knowledge you can use—I've compiled the following *Fog Alert!* list of actual examples from my client work. While some may have hints of problems from other Steps we've discussed, most simply need editing for conciseness. Ready? Here we go!

Step 18
FOG ALERT!

A writer should be concise. The following sentences, selected from manuscripts offered to publishers, contain wordy sentences that cloud meaning and put off readers. Edit them, then check your own manuscripts for similar problems.

Jane inserted her key in the front door and pushed at the often-sticking door, finally giving it a little nudge with her foot.
Jane unlocked the front door and nudged the often-sticking door open with her foot.

Janice moved toward her bedroom, dragging her backpack behind her.
Janice dragged her backpack toward her bedroom.

She dug through the vegetable bin, pulling out some lettuce to make a salad.
She pulled lettuce from the vegetable bin to make a salad.

It's important to deal with these things before they get out of hand.
It's important to deal with these things quickly.

She scraped the remainder of pancakes from Jerry's plate into the garbage.
She scraped Jerry's leftover pancakes into the garbage.

Gloria followed her, and when they entered the office she closed the door.
Gloria followed her into the office and closed the door.

They walked in silence as the sound of singing birds filled the air.
They walked in silence broken only by singing birds.

Betty yawned and then made a casual comment about it being no big deal.
Betty yawned and said it was no big deal.

He thought of the pastries he'd bought on his way home from work.
He thought of the pastries he'd bought after work.

She told him about the dreams that periodically visited her.
She told him about her recurring dreams.

He looked toward the village, but with the mist so thick it was difficult to see it.
He looked toward the village, almost hidden by the thick mist.

I feel that it is most certainly his intention to torture me.
I think he plans to torture me.

They knew there was nothing they could do to protect their people.
They knew they couldn't protect their people.

The look on his face confirmed what she thought.
His expression confirmed her thoughts.

The soldiers stormed the camp and took formation around it.
The soldiers surrounded the camp.

With the exception of those guarding the prisoners, the mounted soldiers dispersed.
The mounted soldiers not guarding the prisoners dispersed.

The felled soldier began screaming out to the others that one of their prisoners was escaping.
"He's escaping!" the felled soldier said.

"You men," he yelled, indicating a small group of soldiers, "come with me. As for the rest of you, go after the others."
He turned to a small group of soldiers. "You men, come with me. The rest go after the others."

YOUR ASSIGNMENT

EDIT THE STEP 18 PROBLEM SENTENCES in the accompanying *Exercise* box and check your work against the *Exercise Solutions* in the appendix.

USE YOUR KNOWLEDGE: Read your Work In Progress, looking for ways to shorten and combine sentences.

Step 18 Exercises

Edit the following sentences as needed and check your work against the *Exercise Solutions* found in the appendix. The number in the parentheses after each line identifies the net number of words you're to eliminate:

18-1: The horse wasn't anywhere to be found. (-3)

18-2: Let's take the horses out by ourselves. (-4)

18-3: She directed most of her comments to Lisa. (-3)

18-4: His thoughts becoming jumbled, Dick tuned them out. (-2)

18-5: She gathered the ingredients she needed for the pancakes. (-4)

18-6: I'm only scheduled for a few hours of work today. (-3)

18-7: Judy drove around with no destination in mind. (-5)

18-8: She found herself unable to move. (-4)

18-9: It was all he could do to maintain his own energy. (-4)

18-10: Her mind was devoid of any thoughts. (-3)

Avoid clichés like the plague

Clichés, trite phrases that once were cutting edge, are a big ingredient in many writers' fog soup. We usually aren't even aware we're using them. Our eyes glaze over as they tumble off our fingertips and into our word processors, unseen. Unseen to us, that is, but a discerning agent or editor notes them. To illustrate a cliché: The next one *you* use may be the one that breaks the camel's back.

Consider this example:

> *Margaret watched Bill out of the corner of her eye.*

Change it to:

> *Margaret secretly watched Bill.*

We've cut verbiage by more than half and improved the sentence.

Our goal is not just to shorten sentences, of course. It's also to give the reader more information. When we use clichés, we're being lazy as writers because it's the easy way out. But our clichés are also generic and don't best show what we're writing about.

The fact is, clichés don't confuse the reader, or make our writing unintelligible. They simply make it boring. We are offering that reader something they've read a thousand times before (note the cliché?), and that's precisely why we should not use clichés.

But beware: Don't substitute clichés with outlandish material that distracts the readers. We don't want to bring them out of their fictional dream.

Step 19
FOG ALERT!

Search for clichés in your work and replace them with your own interpre-
tations, as in the examples below. You can probably come up with much
more creative replacements that add both information and interest.

It was as black as pitch.
It was as black as the inside of an octopus.

He had butterflies in his stomach.
His guts refought World War II.

It was a crushing blow.
The blow could have smashed an atom.

He went from the frying pan to the fire.
Hell swallowed him.

He made it in the nick of time.
He made it before the door slammed shut.

He was none the worse for wear.
He looked like he'd just rolled off the assembly line.

YOUR ASSIGNMENT

EDIT THE STEP 19 PROBLEM SENTENCES in the *Exercise* box below. You'll note that the *Exercise Solutions* listing in the appendix identifies the cliché and leaves a blank for you to insert your own cliché rewrite.

STUDY the more than 200 clichés in the accompanying *Cliché* listing.

TEST YOUR SKILLS: Edit Chapter 8 of *Sarah's Perils* and check your work against *Sarah's Perils Solutions* in the appendix.

USE YOUR KNOWLEDGE: Can you find any clichés in the first chapter of your Work In Progress? If you can, try replacing them with your own creative words.

Step 19 Exercises

Edit the following sentences as needed and check your work against the *Exercise Solutions* listing found in the appendix.

19-1:   The jilted bride was sadder but wiser.

19-2:   It was a real shot in the arm.

19-3:   Boy, that guy's as sly as a fox.

19-4:   Someday my ship will come in.

19-5:   That repair sticks out like a sore thumb.

19-6:   Let's take the bull by the horns.

19-7:   We've been together through thick and thin.

19-8:   Let's not beat around the bush.

19-9:   I'd say that's beyond the realm of possibility.

19-10: He acted like a bull in a china shop.

Avoid clichés like the plague

Following are more than 200 clichés we read and hear every day. Read over the list several times to get them in mind and watch for them in your writing. Each one provides an opportunity to be creative and to pass on new information to your readers.

acid test
after all is said and done
all is fair in love and war
all the world's a stage
all walks of life
aroused our curiosity
as a matter of fact
as blue as the sky
as easy as pie
as smart as a whip
at the blink of an eye
at this point in time
at loose ends
babe in the woods
back to the drawing board
beat around the bush
beauty is only skin deep
behind the eight ball
beyond the realm of possibility
beyond the shadow of a doubt
better late than never
bid farewell
bitter end
blind as a bat
brought back to reality
black as pitch
blind as a bat
bolt from the blue
brutally frank
bull in a china shop
burn the midnight oil
busy as a bee/beaver

butterflies in his stomach
bright and early
by hook or crook
by the same token
calm before the storm
calm, cool, and collected
carve a niche for oneself
cat's meow
checkered career
child's play
choked with emotion
chomping at the bit
cool as a cucumber
cool, calm, and collected
crack of dawn
crushing blow
crying shame
cry over spilt milk
crystal clear
dead as a doornail
depths of despair
dire straits
dog-eat-dog world
don't count your chickens before
    they hatch
don't hold your breath
down but not out
drive one to distraction
drop the ball
dyed in the wool
easier said than done
easy as pie

emotional roller coaster
every cloud has a silver lining
every rose has its thorn
every walk of life
feathered friends
face the music
fall between the cracks
far be it from me
fall on deaf ears
far cry
few and far between
fine and dandy
first and foremost
flash in the pan
flat as a pancake
forever and a day
free and easy
from the frying pan into the fire
from time immemorial
gentle as a lamb
give the devil his due
go at it tooth and nail
good time was had by all
grave danger
greased lightning
green with envy
hang in the balance
happy as a lark
harbinger of the future
haste makes waste
hit the nail on the head
head over heels
heated debate
heavy as lead
high spirits
hone your skills
horns of a dilemma
hour of need

hook, line, and sinker
if you can't beat them, join them
ignorance is bliss
in a nutshell
in any way, shape, or form
in one fell swoop
in the nick of time
in the pipeline
in the same boat
in this day and time
it goes without saying
it's always darkest before the dawn
it stands to reason
keep a stiff upper lip
ladder of success
last but not least
last straw
laughter is the best medicine
leaps and bounds
leave no stone unturned
let's face it
light as a feather
like a ton of bricks
live like a king
lock, stock, and barrel
long arm of the law
looking a gift horse in the mouth
make a clean break/getaway
march of history
meaningful dialogue
method in his madness
moving experience
needle in a haystack
never a dull moment
nipped in the bud
no guts, no glory
no news is good news
none the worse for wear

no pain, no gain
nutty as a fruitcake
off the beaten track
old as the hills
once and for all
one in a million
on the brink of success
open-and-shut case
pain in the _____
parting is such sweet sorrow
patience of Job
pay the piper
playing with fire
pleasingly plump
point with pride
pretty as a picture
pride and joy
pure as newly fallen/driven snow
put it in a nutshell
quick as a flash/wink
quiet as a mouse
rat race
rear its ugly head
ripe old age
rude awakening
rule the roost
rule with an iron fist
sad but true
sadder but wiser
sands of time
screamed like a Banshee
selling like hot cakes
set the world on fire
shot in the arm
shot in the dark
sick as a dog
seize victory from the jaws of
   defeat

sigh of relief
sink or swim
slept like the dead
slept like a log
sly as a fox
slow as molasses
smart as a whip
smooth as silk
sneaking suspicion
sober as a judge
some day my ship will come in
sow one's wild oats
sparked controversy
spread like wildfire
stand in awe
straight as an arrow
straight from the shoulder
stick out like a sore thumb
straw that broke the camel's back
strong as an ox
sweat of their brows
take the bull by the horns
the fact is
the more things change, the more
   they stay the same
the reason being
there is a light at the end of the
   tunnel
this too, shall pass
thin as a rail
throw money around
throughout the length and breadth
through thick and thin
time will tell
tired but happy
to all intents and purposes
to be fair
to be honest

to coin a phrase
today is the first day of the rest of your life
to make a long story short
tomorrow is another day
touch base
tough as nails
trial and error
tried and true
truer words were never spoken
under the weather
until the bitter end
up in arms
vicious circle
wait with bated breath
water over the dam
well-rounded personality
what goes around comes around
when at first you don't succeed, try, try again
when it rains, it pours
when push comes to shove
whirlwind tour
white as a sheet/ghost
winds of change
wise as an owl
work like a dog
worth its weight in gold
wracked his brain
wrapped up in
writing on the wall
you can't tell a book by its cover

CHAPTER 8

SARAH'S PERILS

Sarah slammed the cell phone onto the seat. Damn him! She switched on the radio, and the loud rock-and-roll music from it seemed to be making her even more agitated. She let out a sigh. Even the traffic was as busy as Grand Central Station. She turned left on the other side of the mall to avoid it.

The car in the road ahead of her suddenly stopped in the blink of an eye. Too late, she took her foot off the accelerator and put it on the brake, and pressed hard. Her car skidded on the road beneath her and her car tapped the other's rear bumper. She felt her body go tense.

Her eyes moved over the other car. Apparently, no damage. "Sorry," she called out, as she pulled around it. That damned, lying Joe!

She pondered the phone call. Important to the nation? She needed to try to understand what he meant. She was starting to think that he was being dishonest with her. Joe, Joe, my boy. You're full of it. But I'll get even. You—

And then it hit her, like a bolt from the blue. The perfect solution. After all, all was fair in love and war.

She arrived at her apartment building, pulled into her assigned spot in the parking area, got out, and soon she was in her eighth floor apartment.

Meet her here at eight, huh? Well, okay.

Cool as a cucumber, she walked over to the phone and picked it up and dialed the number for Thompson's Clothing.

Get rid of superficials

Superficials are similar to clichés, which we learned to avoid in Step 19, but there's one big difference. Even though clichés are stilted, they do pass on information. Superficials do not. Many people use them in their speech and writing because they sound like they belong. But if you remove them without replacing them with something else (as we do with clichés) your audience will never miss them.

As an example, consider this sentence:

> *It goes without saying that the sky is a deep blue.*

Compare that with:

> *The sky is a deep blue.*

Don't we see that first clause (It goes without saying that) was unnecessary? It added nothing to the sentence except fog. Yet we hear it, and similar ones, all the time.

The truth is, most superficials are used to "catch our breath." They are space fillers that give us time to think about what we want to say. But they have no place in our writing, which we want to be concise and to flow directly into our reader's brain without filters or barriers.

Step 20
FOG ALERT!

We use some phrases to "catch our breath," both in speaking and writing. They are called *superficials* because they are, well, superficial. The following are examples:

In the final analysis, the first is better than the second.
The first is better than the second.

It goes without saying that I'll be there for you.
I'll be there for you.

It seems that the higher, the better
The higher, the better.

It is important to note that you may need it.
You may need it.

It must be pointed out that it's time for the new one.
It's time for the new one.

I'd like to take this opportunity to thank you.
Thank you.

Please be advised that it's overdue.
It's overdue.

The point I am trying to make is that we may be too late.
We may be too late.

What I mean to say is, we should volunteer.
We should volunteer.

YOUR ASSIGNMENT

EDIT THE STEP 20 PROBLEM SENTENCES in the accompanying *Exercise* box, and compare your work with that in the *Exercise Solutions* listing found in the appendix.

USE YOUR KNOWLEDGE: Search for superficials in your Work In Progress and delete them.

Step 20 Exercises

Edit the following sentences as needed and check your work against the *Exercise Solutions* listing found in the appendix. The number in the parentheses after each line identifies the net number of words you're to eliminate:

20-1:   As you know, this is a Tuesday. (-3)

20-2:   All things considered, it's not a bad choice. (-3)

20-3:   As a matter of fact, it's bigger than the rest. (-5)

20-4:   As far as I'm concerned, you can jump off a cliff. (-5)

20-5:   It's either three or four, as the case may be. (-5)

20-6:   For all intents and purposes, it's a done deal. (-5)

20-7:   For your information, I'm very tired. (-3)

20-8:   In a manner of speaking, it's the biggest frog in the pond. (-5)

20-9:   In a very real sense, it's the better of the two. (-5)

20-10: In my opinion, it tastes great. (-3)

STEP 21

Stop those wandering eyes

Picture this:

> *Her eyes were glued to the TV set.*

No, *really* picture it. Can't you see those two eyes stuck onto the television set, while an eyeless woman sits helplessly across the room? Did someone carry them over and glue them on, or did they roll over by themselves? Or did they....

You get the idea.

We all know the writer meant this:

> *She stared at the TV set.*

But the poor reader is still jolted. That woman just killed her husband. She's turned on the TV to learn if his body has been discovered—all very serious stuff—then the reader snickers at the eyeballs glued to the television. A small point? Not if the reader's concentration is broken.

Often the writer can simply substitute the words "gazed" or "stared" for a phrase like this. Examples are shown in the accompanying *Fog Alert!*

Step 21
FOG ALERT!

Why take a chance? Eliminate roving-eye problems in the following sentences by using "gaze" or "stare."

Her eyes roamed the bar.
She gazed about the bar.

She let her eyes wander up the street.
She gazed up the street.

Her eyes went slowly around the room.
She slowly gazed around the room.

Her eyes went across the road.
She stared across the road.

YOUR ASSIGNMENT

EDIT THE STEP 21 PROBLEM SENTENCES in the *Exercise* box below, and compare your work with that in the *Exercise Solutions* found in the appendix.

TEST YOUR SKILLS: Edit Chapter 9 of *Sarah's Perils* and check your work against *Sarah's Perils Solutions* in the appendix.

USE YOUR KNOWLEDGE: Use your word processor's search function to find the word "eye" in your Work In Progress's first chapter, and think of creative ways to get rid of those wandering eyes.

Step 21 Exercises

Edit the following sentences as needed and check your work against the *Exercise Solutions* found in the appendix. The number in the parentheses after each line identifies the net number of words you're to eliminate. Watch it: There are some trick sentences.

21-1:   Jean's eyes traveled up his slim body. (0)

21-2:   He had his eyes on her all day. (-3)

21-3:   Her eyes followed him. (0)

21-4:   Her eyes took them both in. (0)

21-5:   She couldn't keep her eyes off his body. (-1)

21-6:   Her eyes were drawn to the pictures. (0)

21-7:   He's in the eye of the storm. (0)

21-8:   The eyes of the world are upon you. (0)

21-9:   Her eyes climbed up his body to his face. (0)

21-10: Her eyes traveled about the room and out the window. (0)

CHAPTER 9

SARAH'S PERILS

Sarah licked the pencil tip. Revenge, sweet revenge. Then she put her pencil to the paper and wrote the message: *Joe. The door's unlocked. I have a surprise for you.*

She signed her name, then got some tape and taped the note on the outside of her apartment door. She suddenly looked at her watch. She knew that Joe would be there soon. She just had one more note to write. She went to the table that was by the open balcony door and sat at it and wrote bold letters on a large piece of paper.

Suddenly the elevator door clicked in the hall. She dropped the paper on the carpet by the hall door and then ran into the bedroom. Her eyes traveled back through the crack between the door and the jamb. Suddenly, Joe opened the door and entered.

"Sarah?" He looked down and saw the note, and then he frowned. He picked it up and read it, and slumped. "Oh, God," he was saying. He started to walk toward the balcony, and then he ran out onto it.

Sarah counted. *One, two, three…*

"Sarah!" he suddenly screamed. "God, what did I do?"

Silence. Then he came back in and just kept walking until he was out the hall door. Moments later, the elevator clicked.

It went without saying that he was gone from her life forever.

Sarah then went into the living room and picked up the note. She was smiling as she read it: *"I'm tired of your unfaithfulness. I'm going to jump off the balcony."*

She suddenly walked out onto the balcony and her eyes hit the ground. In the final analysis, the store mannequin did look real. Especially the way its arms and legs were twisted every which way.

Gotcha, Joey baby.

PART THREE

SHARING YOUR WORDS

Sharing your work

Great!

You've applied everything you've learned in the first two parts of this book to your Work In Progress's first chapter. You then gave the rest of your manuscript the same careful treatment.

And now you've finally finished the Great American Novel. No, better than that. You've finished it *and* self-edited it. You've got a book boasting lean, sparking prose and you're ready to send it out. Now comes the next step of your writing adventure.

While finishing a piece of writing rewards the soul, you're not done until you share it with others. What will they think of it? Will they like its twists and turns? In your effort to make sure every word is right, are you sure the story itself will pass the final test of being bought by a publisher? And liked by readers?

Keep in mind that, although you might have self-edited your book perfectly, other problems can keep you from being published. Your story just might not stand up to the scrutiny of discerning readers. Your publishing track record may be weak, a glut of books on the same topic may have established a permanent residence on bookstore shelves, or a publisher's editor might just be having a bad day. All of these can affect a manuscript's reception.

Is your book ready for prime time? Now's the time to find out.

CHAPTER **11**

Critique partners

Your first step, if you haven't already taken it, is to find a critique partner who understands your writing and goals.

That's not your spouse, because he/she loves you and thinks anything you do is perfect—at least it's nice to think so! A good friend might shower you with compliments, but a good critique partner will point out writing problems you might not see.

You may have already met writers who would love to critique your work if you critique theirs. This arrangement can provide honest input to your writing and exposure to *their* writing techniques and problems. You'll see things you might want to do and not do in your own work.

Most published writers have a critique partner; many have two or three. Your writing can achieve a whole new level when other writers point out things you're doing wrong. You can also be proactive and ask about scenes you're planning to write and those that aren't going well.

Finding a critique partner

There are several ways to find good critique partners. Some national writers' organizations have online critique groups for members, and you can post your critique needs on their message boards or discuss them in forums. Also, check with local writing groups and continuing education writing classes at local universities.

Some writers' organizations also sponsor contests that provide feedback from savvy judges, and they can be both invaluable and inexpensive. I've entered some and judged others, and I find them to be one of the best short-term critiquing methods around.

In your search for a critique partner, consider local writers' groups, including chapters of national writers' organizations. If you're not aware of any, check with local libraries, bookstores, and college English departments. Writers often meet at such sites on a monthly or bi-monthly basis and read hard copy pages of each others' work, and sometimes read their own pages in front of the group. You may be nervous the first time you read pages, but soon you'll settle in and actually enjoy the experience.

Finally, put a notice on Facebook or Twitter or respond to such notices. You'll find requests for reading queries, synopses, and chapters.

Remember, just because someone calls herself a writer doesn't make her a good critique partner candidate. When you find likely prospects, make sure they're aware of the publishing industry's ups and down and are familiar with your genre, the market, and the general business of writing. If their opinions aren't based on experience and education, you can't be sure their comments are on target. Also, make sure your critique partner's personality meshes with yours. She should be able to point out specific areas of concern without making you feel small and stupid.

Search the Internet

You say you still can't find someone who might critique your work? Or, that these techniques didn't turn up qualified reading partners? Not to worry. Just remember: The Internet is your friend.

Some writers find critique partners by traveling through the blogosphere and reading blogs written by writers in their genre. Bloggers occasionally post that they're looking for a critique partner. If you find one who is knowledgeable in your genre and would be a good fit for you, ask that person if they're interested in partnering.

But that's just the tip of the online critique-partner iceberg. If you Google "critique partners online," you'll get—count them—more than nine million hits. I'm confident you'll find a critique partner who fits your exact needs on the first two or three pages of your search results.

Some sites you'll find exist solely to match up critique partners in almost any genre. You can make a match either by responding to another writer's query, in which she describes her goals, writing level, and so on, or you can throw out your own bait and wait for responses.

Critique sites work in various ways. On some, you upload your work (a chapter, say) and anyone can critique it and return it to you. This can become a problem, since you may get five responses and are then expected to critique material from all five writers. You might find yourself spending more time critiquing than writing.

Follow these unwritten rules

Whatever method you use to find a critique partner, remember these unwritten rules:

1. Critiquing is a two-way street. You must read their pages, too.
2. Start off small, with just a chapter or two. If you like the critique, you can always send more.
3. Set the ground rules early. How fast should the turnaround be? How much material, how often? Are there any particular things you want your partner to look for? Any others you don't really care about? Worried about your point of view? Your characters' development? Let your prospective partner know exactly what you want, and you'll avoid conflict later.
4. Don't argue with your partner about her findings. If you think they're wrong, just ignore them. If they're wrong too often, end the relationship.

Selecting a critique partner isn't as important as selecting a spouse, but it's up there. There's a courtship period in either relationship. Make sure you both agree on the basics before you start, and your lives will be much easier if you have to part.

YOUR ASSIGNMENT

Quietly study your writing friends, especially those who have been published, to see if they would make good critique partners. Expand your search to include members of local and national writing groups. If you still come up with nothing, search the Internet for "critique partners online."

CHAPTER **12**

Professional editors

Critique partners are useful. But should you also have your writing edited by a professional before sending to a publisher or agent?

The short answer is, absolutely.

Years ago, it wasn't so important, since publishers had more editors on staff than they do now. But that has gone the way of the buggy whip. Even though your writing has gotten your critique partner's approval, it probably still needs a great deal of work in order to make it publishable. I know that firsthand, from both my experience as a contest judge and as a professional editor.

Let's discuss the contests first. Realize that the contestants have worked hard on their entries, generally up to twenty pages or so, polishing them to within an inch of their lives. Their critique partners have blessed them, and they have now paid to see what more experienced writers think of their work.

The problem? The judges' marks generally fall far short of what the writers expect.

Remember, those entries reflect the best writing they can do. They've sweated tears over them and huddled at their post office boxes or their computers waiting for the judging results. Remember, also, that these are only the first few pages of a two- to four-hundred page manuscript and that the rest of the pages didn't get the same loving care the entry did. That means the remainder of the manuscript is probably in worse shape than that first chapter.

But I'm also aware that most writers' work needs editing because I see the proof every day as I edit for others. I get many of my editing assignments through a network with a big presence on the Internet that asks potential clients to send fifty pages of their manuscript for evaluation. I've seen hundreds of proposals to edit.

Just as they do with contest entries, writers send editing agencies the most polished writing possible. While I have passed on a handful believing they were almost good enough to go as is, I have passed on many more because they were not nearly ready for editing, and the writer couldn't afford to pay an editor to do the massive amount of work needed. The rest needed moderate to heavy editing.

Publishers and agents are literary gatekeepers who vet your work before a reader sees it. If a novel needs editing, in most cases they'll pass on it, and its writer will send it to another editor. And another and another and another.... As I said in this book's introduction, some writers will never be published, and they won't know why. A qualified freelance editor will easily spot the problems and give the author a heads-up that might turn a stream of rejections into a writing career.

The model's changing

The need for professional editing is greater now than ever before. For hundreds of years, the industry model has been from writer to publisher (or agent) and finally to reader. But now we're in the midst of a publishing revolution, where writers can bypass these traditional gatekeepers and go directly to the public through online distributors like Amazon.com and BarnesandNoble.com. Suddenly, it seems, anyone can be published without all those rejection slips. That's a good thing, right?

Well, maybe. It just depends.

Remember, we've killed off the gatekeepers, and now both our great and our garbled manuscripts go freely through those gates into the readers' hands. If readers find garbage instead of a well-crafted story, they spread the word. They have assumed the gatekeeper's role and pour boiling oil on our sales in two ways. If they read a free sample of our virtual book and the writing is flawed, they simply won't buy it. If they do buy a book and find it's not been edited, they'll warn others by posting scathing reviews on Amazon, Barnes & Noble, or wherever they bought the book. As a comedian once said, readers will then stay away in droves. And, they'll stay away from every book you publish the rest of your life, unless it's been edited properly.

Finding a qualified editor

So, how do you find an editor? Well, the same way you find a critique partner—by word of mouth and on the Internet. Be warned, though, that you need to be your *own* gatekeeper when you select an editor. Just because someone says they're a freelance editor doesn't mean they are a good one or, in fact, have the qualities to make them even a mediocre one.

Let me tell you horror stories I'm personally aware of. A friend wrote a book that was accepted by a small traditional publisher, who sent it to their freelance editor. My friend waited for months, listening to the editor's reasons for not doing anything. Finally, the publisher assigned the author to another editor, and she also proceeded to prove her worth lay elsewhere. Her idea of editing was to switch the sequence of scenes for no apparent reason. She explained to a mutual acquaintance, "I generally edit a book a week." While I have no problem with editors working fast, her clients certainly weren't getting a quality editing job.

I've had bad editors myself. An online publisher sent my manuscript to a freelance editor who told me my points of view were all screwed up. But they weren't! I saw clearly she had no clue about what she was doing and we soon parted company.

There are ways, of course, to ensure the editor you hire is capable. First, get references. What does that friend in your writing club say about the editor she hired? If she likes her work and recommends her, ask her if she'll let you see a sample of that person's work. If you like what you see, go for it.

A good source for editor information is the Editorial Freelancers Association (www.the-efa.org). Here you'll find a membership directory broken down by skills and specialties. There are background listings for hundreds of fiction editors. The site also lists common rates, broken down by the type of work needed. Individual editors' fees vary, of course.

While there are many qualified editors on the Internet, there are also those who one day said, "I are a editor, too," and hung their virtual shingle. Read their websites carefully, and if you like what you see, ask for client names and email addresses. Follow up to see what the clients think of that editor's work.

A good bet, I think, is to consider an online editing network whose editors have passed rigorous editing tests (its website should tell you this), since it can serve as a gatekeeper that assures you a quality editor. You'll be asked to provide basic information about your writing, including a short synopsis and the first fifty pages of your manuscript. Such a network's website features pages of editors' profiles, and you can select one or let the network's personnel select for you. The chosen editor will read your material and, if he's interested, contact you within hours via email. He may offer to send you a sample edit of your work that will show you his skills firsthand. Your contract will be with him, not the network.

Editing is serious business. It takes time and experience and, done properly, will help give your readers an experience they'll enjoy and tell others about. This is one of those areas where "you get what you pay for," and a too-cheap price could identify an editor who knows little and will not give your work the time and treatment it deserves.

YOUR ASSIGNMENT

Visit the Editorial Freelancers Association website (the-efa.org) and study its members' listings and fees. Go online to a professional editing network that tests its editors and read the qualifications of those listed. Compare them with local editors and those found elsewhere on the Internet that interest you. When you find good prospects, check with their clients for references and to see what they think of their work. Remember: A cheap editing rate doesn't always go hand in hand with quality editing.

CHAPTER 13

Publishers and agents

Finding your target publishers

You've written a book, edited it, had your critique partner go over it, and even had a professional editor polish it. What now?

Well, you're ready to approach a publisher.

You probably have a target publisher or two in mind. You've obviously read in your genre and are basically familiar with the publishers whose books you like.

If you haven't yet identified your targets, or are not familiar with them, do a quick horseback research at your local big-box bookstore, such as Barnes and Noble and Books-A-Million. Go to the shelves holding books in your genre and, starting at one end and continuing to the other, study them. Jot down every publisher's name and read blurbs and first pages you want to emulate. Immerse yourself. You'll probably find more publishers than you realized existed and may find one that's a better fit for the story you've written than the one you'd previously targeted. When you leave the store, you should have a long list of publishers to check out.

Another great source for publisher's information is the annual *Writers Market*, published by *Writers Digest* magazine. It's packed with directories of publishers and agents, plus many useful articles by published authors, agents, and editors. It's well worth the small investment.

Now, visit those publishers' websites and note what they're looking for. (You can find them by Googling the publisher's name.) Click on tabs marked "Submissions" and read carefully. The trick in genre writing—or any writing, for that matter—is to offer publishers exactly what they want. Publishers (and imprints within publishing companies) specialize in different kinds of books, so it pays to be attentive to this. Outside of genre writing, most publishers don't have stringent guidelines about character types or writing patterns, but, of course, it's useless to send your novel to an imprint that publishes cookbooks.

Another way to find publishers is to Google "book publisher directories." You'll find several legitimate directories that will help you in your search. You'll also find companies who say they want to publish your book, but run the other way. Many are "vanity publishers"—that is, publishing houses that charge authors to have their books published. You certainly don't need that.

Also, check to see if a national writing group you belong to has a listing of publishers they think are legitimate.

Finding and working with publishers is similar to finding and working with the agents who provide publishers with manuscripts, so we'll cover both at one time below. In most instances, you can interchange "agent" for "publisher."

Finding an agent

While some publishers will accept submissions directly from writers, many will not. They ask for "agent submissions only," and that means you can't personally submit to them. They know agents will have made sure your story fits their needs and is well written and edited. So, an agent is the publisher's gatekeeper.

How do you find an agent? Your best source is the Internet.

While there are certainly other sources—type "literary agencies" into Google or another search site and you'll be amazed at how many pop up—I personally recommend a site called AgentQuery.com. This site offers the largest, most current searchable database of literary agents on the web. And, it's free.

Select your genre from the list provided, then click a "quick search" button that takes you to a section containing thumbnails of all the literary agencies that handle that genre. Each presents brief facts about a given agency. Here you can learn, among other things, if an agency is currently accepting submissions, and whether it accepts email queries. One is tempted to select only those of the latter type, but AgentQuery.com points out that some of the snail-mail-only agents often make good sales to publishers with deep pockets. My own plan would be to send to those who accept email queries first.

When you find agents that look interesting, click on the "Full Profile" eye icon to be transported to their full listing, which includes submission guidelines, full addresses, whether or not they accept simultaneous submissions, and so on. These sites are agent-specific; that is, they are not about the agency itself, but about an individual at the agency. You can learn that person's special interests and what she doesn't want. One, for example, says: "She is only seeking women's fiction, romance, and young adult genres. In terms of women's fiction, she likes a good cry; she's more a *Steel Magnolias* kind of girl than a *Sex & the City* type, and she likes Southern fiction." This page also describes recent books she's placed with publishers.

Submitting to an agent

Okay, you've selected ten agents you want to approach. Now's the time to show them how professional you are.

The fiction submission process depends on what a particular agent wants. There is no such thing as a "standard submission process." All agents and publishers require a query letter, and that's all some will accept in your initial contact. Others want more up-front, such as a synopsis and possibly the first twenty pages or the first two or three chapters. Send only what a particular publisher or agent asks for. If they're interested, they'll tell you what to send next. *Never send the full manuscript until asked for it, but be sure you've finished it before making contact.* If agents ask to see your manuscript, you can be sure they'll lose interest fast if you can't send it.

Children's picture books are different, since they're so short. Agencies want the full manuscript up front. But don't send illustrations or make your own unless you're a professional illustrator. Usually, publishers will match artists with authors.

Now you're ready to contact the agents on your list. I suggest that you select ten agents who accept simultaneous submissions—that is, those who don't mind if you send to other agents at the same time. They realize it's simply not fair for you to wait for months while your manuscript languishes in their slush pile and that it could take you years to present your manuscript to ten agents, one after another. Some agents (and publishers) demand that you send to them exclusively, but why would you want to?

Now, carefully study their needs. Craft a basic query letter (see Chapter 14), personalize it for each specific agent, and send it out to all ten selected agents who allow simultaneous submissions. But don't send out more than ten at a time. It's possible you'll get valuable feedback from an agent rejecting your work, and you'll want to redo your query letter before you send it out again. Also, you might want to redo the query letter if you don't hear from any agents, since it may have a basic flaw. If you don't get a positive response from any in two or three months—shorter for an emailed query—send out another ten query letters to different agents.

YOUR ASSIGNMENT

Go online to AgentQuery.com and select ten agents who handle your genre and allow simultaneous submissions. Study their needs carefully, paying particular attention to what they want from you. Send specifically what each of the ten agents wants to receive.

CHAPTER 14

Writing the query letter

The query letter is your pitch to the publisher or agent. Since what you say in it will affect whether or not you'll be published, it's certainly worth spending time on. Writing an intelligent, intriguing query will prompt an agent to ask for more and move you closer to a book sale.

Three ingredients

Although queries sound scary, they are actually quite simple in structure. Like manuscript formats, they have evolved to a standard form expected by every agent or publisher. Once we realize that, our job is easier.

First, a cardinal rule: *Every query for fiction should be single-spaced on a single page.* Squeezing all your good points onto that page might seem daunting, but it's well worth doing. You want to catch that busy agent's attention quickly, and he'll be turned off by a longer query.

A proper query letter has three concise sections: the hook and mini-synopsis, your biography, and the closing. You can see these sections in the accompanying sample query letter (Fig. 14-1), which I used to sell one of my own books.

Your query letter hook works the same as those hooks we discussed in Chapter 2. You want to hook that reader—in this case an agent or publisher—in the first paragraph. One way to set your hook is to begin your query letter with the word "When," and reveal an event, the main character, conflict, and triumph. It's an age-old formula that works. Following are two examples from successful queries I've written. The first is for *BJ, Milo, and the Hairdo from Heck*:

When twenty-something hairdresser BJ Stalnaker parlays her half of modest lottery winnings into an international hairdo business and her husband Milo's brand-new franchise schemes go into the dumper, sparks fly. His recently departed daddy said he was supposed to earn all his family's bread! They're re-united in a heartwarming conclusion by a wheel-shaped church, a "hairdo from heck," actions of an oddball set of characters, and separate epiphanies.

Note that I provide the story's meat, but also leave hints of good things to come.

The second example is from the query for *Mystery at Magnolia Mansion*:

When Brenda Maxwell's new interior design client tells her to "paint, wallpaper, whatever" his hundred-year-old landmark mansion, she figures her grandiose plans will fit handily into his edict's "whatever" section and launches them into a constant head-bumping mode.

Her poor money management skills (that's his view, but what does he know?) and lawyer David Hasbrough's ridiculous need to control her life (that's her well-reasoned evaluation of the situation) combine to keep the battle going. Add a dollop of "the other woman's" interference, throw in secrets about the house and both their pasts, fold in a dab of parental abuse and a pinch of good old-fashioned mistrust, and you have a recipe for disaster. Is this couple's romantic goose cooked?

Notice that I've written both in a playful voice, the same as used for the stories themselves.

The second section of your query letter presents your qualifications to write the book. Here, you tell about your published writing, writing programs you've attended, and writing-related organizations you belong to. Don't include non-pertinent information, such as the fact that you are a birdwatcher or that all three of your children are doctors, unless this information is relevant to your story.

You say you have no publishing credits? That's not a problem. You can tell briefly why you became interested in the subject, how you researched it, and why it's so important. Here's an example from the query letter of one of my non-published clients who wrote a great adventure story:

> *I wrote this book because it answers my own need for excitement. I've been a fixed-wing pilot, commercial helicopter pilot and flight instructor, commercial diver, professional dog trainer for retrievers, self-employed entrepreneur, commercial crab fisherman in Alaska, and a trained assassin.*

How could an agent not be interested?

And, here's one more example of a non-published writer's bio that will attract agent attention:

> *The novel, titled _____, is a 96,500-word thriller. I started writing it when I was laid off nearly three years ago, and soon realized losing my job was a real opportunity to change course. I took copywriting and feature writing classes, but fiction has always been my love. I've worked closely with a book editor this past year to make this book the best it can possibly be.*

This short query bio shows sincerity and dedication, and especially the fact that a professional editor oversaw her book's development. Agents will appreciate the fact that a gatekeeper has helped her and has given it his implied approval.

I quickly point out that many editors have a policy against letting clients use their name in such letters and the acknowledgements section of their books, since there's always a chance clients will re-edit and introduce mistakes the editor doesn't want to own. But mentioning such a person's involvement is a good marketing idea.

The final section is your closing. Here's where you thank the agent for her time and consideration, let her know the full manuscript is available, tell her you've enclosed a self-addressed stamped envelope (if you're querying by snail mail), and ask her for the order.

Now, read your query letter over to make sure you've included all the basics. Have you addressed a specific agent? Did you provide your book's title? Did you mention its word count and genre? Did you list your contact phone number and email address? You'd be surprised at how many writers forget this basic information.

YOUR ASSIGNMENT

Write your query letter, following the guidelines above, and have your critique partner or a friend proofread it.

Figure 14-1: Sample Query Letter

Don McNair

Street Address, City, State, Zip
Tel: 251/333-3333 • myemailaddress.com

(Date)
Jane Doe
XYZ Publishing Company
123 Main Street
City, State, Zip

Dear Ms. Doe:

When antiques dealer Erica Phillips inspects choice property inherited from a father she never knew existed, she finds scientist Mike Cleverdon camped there to study unique, soon-to-be-hatched fireflies. She must sell the property to afford a new business location, but he freaks out when a condo builder makes her an offer. She tells him, "If I have my way, this place will be sold within the week. And, Mr. Cleverdon, I will have my way!"

That's all in the first chapter of *Mystery on Firefly Knob*, a 60,000-word romance novel I hope you'll want to publish. The book shows their ups and downs and ends as they identify and subdue her father's killers, view the remarkable insects, and realize their love is forever.

I've written five published novels: two young adult (*Attack of the Killer Prom Dresses* and *The Long Hunter*), two romantic suspense (*Mystery at Magnolia Mansion*, and co-authored *Waiting for Backup!*), and a romantic comedy (*BJ, Milo, and the Hairdo from Heck*). I've also written and placed hundreds of trade magazine articles and three published non-fiction, how-to books.

I've supported my family by writing and editing all my working life. I edited trade magazines for twelve years, was a PR account executive for six, and headed my own PR firm for twenty-one. My creativity won three Golden Trumpets from the Publicity Club of Chicago and the PRSA's Silver Anvil, their version of an Oscar or Emmy.

But that's all in the past. I now concentrate on writing novels and editing for others, and would welcome a contract for this and other books yet to come. I enclose a synopsis, three chapters, and a SASE, and look forward to hearing from you!

Cordially,
Don McNair

CHAPTER 15

Writing the synopsis

Now comes one of the toughest jobs of all—stuffing that two- to four-hundred-page manuscript into a two- to twenty-page synopsis. At least it seems that way as you face a blank page on your word processor.

The synopsis is an important selling tool, and you should have yours ready before you send out your query letter. In some cases, an agent will want them sent together. It's an outline, a narrative summary of your book. Think of it as a way to tell your friends the novel's plot, and it may not be so scary.

If an agent likes your query letter, she'll ask for a synopsis and perhaps sample pages. The synopsis will let her know what your characters' conflicts are, how you've built them throughout the story, and whether they'll hold the reader's attention to the end. She also wants to know whether or not your novel meets her genre's specific requirements.

As a guide, I've presented a synopsis which helped me sell *Mystery on Firefly Knob* when a publisher responded to the query letter found in Chapter 14. You'll find this sample synopsis in the Appendix.

Check the individual publisher's and editor's submission guidelines. Some want to see a twenty-page synopsis, and others want only a two-page synopsis. If no particular length is requested, you're safe if you send one that is ten pages or so long. It's relatively easy to boil it down to a two-page or five-page document for those who request that length.

Don't get heavily into descriptions. That is, don't say things like "she had a tawny complexion and black curly hair that cascaded over her shoulders." You don't have room for it. And, leave out secondary characters, unless they are important to the plot and affect the main characters.

Format your synopsis the same as you formatted your manuscript. That is, double-spaced, with one-inch margins, and in the same font. Use the same header (author last name/book title), but add the word "synopsis." Also add page numbers at the top right.

As with query letters, synopses follow a proven pattern. They're written in omniscient present tense, for example, and in third person. And, they're written in the same voice the book is. If your story is somber, your synopsis should be, too. If it's light in tone, so should be the synopsis.

Don't get bogged down in details, or your synopsis will be way too long. Just introduce your characters and hit the book's high points. You obviously don't want to include every character, subplot, or scene, but you do want the publisher and agent to understand what happens to the main characters, what their crises are, and how they solve their problems. Make sure your narrative transitions easily from one idea to the next.

Be sure to show how the novel ends. New writers sometimes leave that information out, believing the agent will want to know how it turns out and will therefore ask for the manuscript. That trick has probably never worked, and it certainly lets the agent know she's working with an amateur.

Basic composition

Start your synopsis with a paragraph that presents a clear, brief view of your main character, showing the situation he/she's in when your story opens. In the next paragraph, show what triggers the story's main conflict. You'll recall in our discussion on hooks (Chapter 2), that this is the story question. It's the first shoe being dropped.

Next, present the sequence of events in your novel. Don't try to summarize each chapter, because that doesn't work. For one thing, you'll wind up with a fifty-page tome. Simply read the chapter and "tell" your word processor what's in it, as if you're telling your best friend about a movie you saw last night. Leave out adjectives, adverbs, and physical descriptions. That lake might shimmer in the moonlight when the cool breeze blows in from over the rye field, but let the agent find that out when (we hope!) she reads the manuscript. Also, don't include dialogue. You may want to occasionally inject a strong quote from a character, but keep it brief.

Finally, wrap up the story in the final paragraph. This is where you resolve the main conflict.

One more point. If an agent asks to see your manuscript, be sure to write "requested material" on the envelope or in the subject line of an email. This will assure that it bypasses the slush pile and lands quickly on her desk, or doesn't vanish with the depression of a "delete" key.

Now it's up to you

Well, that's it, folks. I've been a writer and editor for fifty years, and have enjoyed sharing my story with you. I hope what I've said will help you become a published writer many times over.

I predict your trip to being published will be good, indeed. You've taken the first step by buying this book. Your next step should be to apply what you've learned here to everything you write. Keep this book next to your computer and apply its chapters and Steps, one by one, as you edit. Many others have been enthused with their results of doing so, and I'm sure you will be, too.

Who knows? Maybe I'll see your name on the next best seller!

Appendix

EXERCISE SOLUTIONS

Following are solutions to the exercise problems you were presented throughout this book. The struck-out words are to be taken out, and words in parentheses are to be added.

Step 1

1-1:   It ~~was growing~~ (grew) larger as she watched.

1-2:   She ~~was hoping~~ (hoped) they would stop.

1-3:   Something ~~was troubling~~ (troubled) Susan.

1-4:   Betty ~~was hoping~~ (hoped) they'd change the subject.

1-5:   She ~~was wearing~~ (wore) a white T-shirt.

1-6:   But something ~~was stopping~~ (stopped) her.

1-7:   He ~~was wearing~~ (wore) the same clothes he'd worn last night.

1-8:   (No change)

1-9:   ~~Retracing~~ (Jackie retraced) her steps (and) ~~Jackie~~ found the handkerchief.

1-10:   ~~Looking~~ (Georgia looked disappointed that Sarah had guessed~~, Georgia said,~~.) "You're right."

Step 2

2-1:   She ~~started to drive~~ (drove) toward the setting sun.

2-2:   The landlord ~~decided to increase~~ (increased) Jackie's rent, making her bill-paying sessions real challenges.

2-3: She watched the doorknob ~~start to~~ turn.

2-4: Jane didn't ~~seem to~~ dwell on Susan's actions. "It's already done," she said.

2-5: The trees whizzed by as Max ~~started to run~~ (ran) toward the cabin.

2-6: "~~I'm going to~~ (I'll) tell you."

2-7: "~~We're going to~~ (We'll) get out of here."

2-8: "What ~~are you going to be doing~~ (will you do) while you wait for us?"

2-9: "~~I'm~~ (I) definitely ~~not going to~~ (won't) do something like that."

2-10: Large padlocks ensured no one ~~was going to~~ (would) use those stairs in either direction.

Step 3

3-1: The (boy threw the) ball ~~was thrown by the boy~~.

3-2: ~~Was~~ (Did) Mary ~~the recipient of~~ (receive) the award?

3-3: ~~The game was won by~~ Team B (won the game).

3-4: (The fall killed) Jackie ~~was killed by the fall~~.

3-5: The ~~tree was felled by the~~ lumberjack (felled the tree).

3-6: (A) ~~The beds were made by a~~ hotel employee (made the bed).

3-7: The ~~team was defeated by the~~ Tuscaloosa Raiders (defeated the team).

3-8: ~~The~~ (Find the) answer ~~is found~~ by dividing by pi.

3-9: The (chef burned the) toast ~~was burned by the chef~~.

3-10: The ~~show was cancelled by the~~ committee (cancelled the show).

Step 4

4-1: ~~There were twelve~~ (Twelve) students (were) in the class.

4-2: ~~There is no one~~ (John is) working (alone) ~~with John~~.

4-3: ~~There were several~~ (Several) angry people ~~at~~ (attended) the rally.

4-4:   ~~There are many~~ (Many) vacant lots ~~that~~ need our attention.

4-5:   The ~~boy had a~~ (boy's) dog ~~that~~ was smaller than mine.

4-6:   I ~~had a dream~~ (dreamed) ~~that~~ Paul kissed me.

4-7:   ~~She wore a~~ (Her) red dress ~~that~~ touched the floor.

4-8:   ~~There are many~~ (Many) plates ~~that~~ are prettier.

4-9:   ~~There were~~ (Some) people ~~that~~ liked it.

4-10: ~~He had a~~ (His) horse ~~that~~ was wild.

Step 5

5-1:   They had spent the night walking along the beach. She ~~had~~ wondered if he felt the same way she did.

5-2:   Herbert had kissed her cheek. ~~Hadn't he known~~ (Didn't he know) she was spoken for?

5-3:   Had he suspected? She ~~had known~~ (knew) he was watching her.

5-4:   ~~Hadn't he realized~~ (Didn't he realize) she was pregnant?

5-5:   Surely he ~~had come~~ (came) ready to fight.

5-6:   ~~Had~~ (Were) the tables ~~been~~ lined up properly?

5-7:   ~~Had~~ (Was) the car ~~been~~ parked in the right place?

5-8:   The store ~~had been~~ (was) closed for the season.

5-9:   She ~~had~~ asked if she could have the pink one.

5-10: The box ~~had been~~ (was) empty when they left.

Step 6

6-1:   Maxine ~~would be able to~~ (could) close the shop in March.

6-2:   Janice ~~would~~ (could) certainly ~~be able to~~ swing the deal.

6-3:   Bob (could) ~~would~~ have ~~been able to score~~ (scored) the point.

6-4:   Tom felt he ~~would be able to~~ (could) do it.

6-5:   ~~Would~~ (Could) he ~~be able to~~ climb it?

6-6:   John ~~would be able to~~ (could) win the contest, hands down.

6-7: He probably ~~wouldn't have been able to do~~ (couldn't have done) it on time.

6-8: Jim ~~had the ability to~~ (could) excel in sports.

6-9: Betty ~~had the skills to~~ (could) pull it off.

6-10: ~~Did~~ (Could) he have ~~the knowledge to pass~~ (passed) the test?

Step 7

7-1: She ~~looked up and~~ followed the flashlight beam.

7-2: The stream ~~widened and~~ formed a pool.

7-3: John ~~turned and~~ looked back at Jack.

7-4: Someone must have ~~come and~~ towed it away.

7-5: Emily ~~reached out and~~ grabbed his arm.

7-6: Would you ~~get~~ (lay) the blanket ~~and lay it~~ out over there?

7-7: Please ~~pick up~~ (answer) the phone ~~and answer it~~.

7-8: Let's ~~open~~ (drink) that cola ~~and drink it~~.

7-9: She ~~reached over and~~ petted the lamb.

7-10: Would you please ~~open the door and~~ leave the apartment?

Step 8

8-1: We must keep those funds separate ~~and distinct~~.

8-2: Let's let the guests ~~mix and~~ mingle.

8-3: Well, he's certainly ~~hale and~~ hearty.

8-4: I honestly ~~and truthfully~~ believe that.

8-5: He had various ~~and sundry~~ reasons.

8-6: The reasons are many ~~and varied~~.

8-7: Let's pick up the ~~bits and~~ pieces.

8-8: The plain ~~and simple~~ fact is that it's too big.

8-9: Let's ~~pick and~~ choose among the possibilities.

8-10: I want a full ~~and complete~~ accounting.

Step 9

9-1: He ~~gave an address to~~ (addressed) the audience.

9-2: Joanne ~~took a sip of~~ (sipped) her drink.

9-3: I'm going to ~~put a halt to~~ (stop) that immediately.

9-4: I'll ~~take satisfaction in~~ (enjoy) watching it.

9-5: Come back when I've ~~made up my mind~~ decided.

9-6: He ~~took exception to~~ (challenged) my reasoning.

9-7: You should (consider) ~~take~~ that ~~under advisement~~.

9-8: The police (arrested) ~~took~~ him ~~into custody~~.

9-9: There ~~is a wide range of~~ (are many) options.

9-10: Let's do it ~~at this point in time~~ (now).

Step 10

10-1: (Betty's) ~~Betty felt her~~ heart ~~sink~~ (sank).

10-2: He was trying to trick her~~, she thought~~.

10-3: ~~She saw that the~~ The sky was gray.

10-4: ~~They could see a~~ (A) dozen or so children (were) playing with toys.

10-5: ~~I know you'll~~ (You'll) be sorry if you don't.

10-6: ~~I guess~~ I'd better go check the food.

10-7: ~~I think he's~~ (He's) afraid to be around when you do it.

10-8: ~~Jerry felt the~~ (The) weight ~~press~~ (pressed) down on him.

10-9: ~~I think you'd~~ (You'd) be better off without him.

10-10: He was messing with her mind~~, she thought~~.

Step 11

11-1: "How good of you to come," he said ~~solicitously~~.

11-2: "Uh, we're from the Bar M ranch," Nancy (said) ~~explained haltingly~~.

11-3: "Well, I just wanted to try it," Matt said ~~sheepishly~~.

11-4: "Hey, you know what?" George said ~~excitedly~~.

11-5: "After that, you can do what you want," she said ~~coaxingly~~.

11-6: "Get off that horse, or else!" he said ~~angrily~~.

11-7: "Why, that's the sweetest thing I've ever seen," she said ~~approvingly~~.

11-8: "Who owns that horse?" he asked~~, wondering~~.

11-9: "I'd say there were about eleven of them," he said~~, estimating~~.

11-10: "Good lord, they're coming our way!" he said~~, anxiously~~.

Step 12

12-1: "Let's get out of here," he ~~urged~~ (said).

12-2: "I suppose we could do it that way," he ~~hedged~~ (said).

12-3: "You must go with me!" he ~~demanded~~ (said).

12-4: "It was probably the one on the left," he ~~guessed~~ (said).

12-5: "We probably should leave," he ~~suggested~~ (said).

12-6: "That was funny," he ~~laughed~~ (said).

12-7: "Is that the right one?" he ~~wondered~~ (said).

12-8: "Leave me alone!" he ~~shouted~~ (said).

12-9: "Would you like one?" he ~~queried~~ (said).

12-10: "I see you picked the right one," he ~~observed~~ (said).

Step 13

13-1: (Mike glanced at her, then back at the road.) "Wonder what?" ~~Mike asked finally.~~

13-2: (Mike pulled over and stopped.) "My turn to play tour director~~;~~(.)" ~~Mike said.~~

13-3: (He was silent for a moment.) "Well, yesterday~~," Mike said~~. They have to have twenty-four hours' notice."

13-4: (Jean stood, showing a body obviously used to exercise.) "We'll loan you one~~," she said~~. Where will you be working?"

13-5: (A weak smile brightened his otherwise dour face.) "Would you really sell that land to a condo developer?" ~~he asked.~~

190

13-6: (His smile broadened.) "Oh, but you're wrong,~~" he said.~~ It's every bit my business."

13-7: (Mike glared at her.) "It means you need to tell me what I did wrong~~.~~(.)"~~ Mike said.~~

13-8: (She looked up at him.) "Did you read the editorial?" ~~she asked.~~

13-9: (He stepped to her.) "You've got to believe me~~,~~(.)" ~~he said.~~

13-10: (Mike eyed his father.) "You've picked up some weight~~,~~(.)" ~~Mike said.~~

Step 14

14-1: "The ~~urgent nature of the~~ invitations(' urgent nature) was unusual~~., we know, asking~~ (We asked) you to interrupt your work, your vacation, ~~or~~ (and) in one case, a planned surgery. (If you) ~~In the case of those who~~ didn't respond quickly and affirmatively ~~to our invitation~~, we reluctantly (pressured) ~~put a little bit of pressure on~~ your organization. (Ninety-seven percent of those invited are here.) ~~We have a 97% success rate for attracting attendees who were in our initial solicitation.~~ (We have alternates for) ~~In place of~~ the five people who thought this was just so much hype~~, we have alternates in those fields joining us today.~~"

14-2: "At first we thought ~~that~~ this might be a (fallen) satellite ~~that re-entered the Earth's atmosphere~~, but there ~~were no signs of~~ (was no re-entry) scorching ~~associated with re-entry~~ (or impact damage). ~~In fact, there were no signs at all of damaged caused by heat or by impact. Then we thought it might be a bomb that was inadvertently dropped, but it seemed too~~ (Was it a bomb? No, it seemed too) large and irregularly shaped~~ to resemble a bomb or warhead.~~"

Step 15

15-1: "You sure?" ~~He seemed a little uncertain.~~

15-2: "John!" Sarah ~~looked~~ (stared) at him~~ in alarm.~~

15-3:   "Who cares?" ~~Bob waved that problem aside~~.

15-4:   "Are you back on that Phil kick again?" Sarah asked~~, her tone hostile~~.

15-5:   "I didn't know it was a sensitive issue," Kermit said~~, as if in surrender~~.

15-6:   "This is (a) ~~an authentic~~ replica."

15-7:   "I'm convinced it was ~~deliberate~~ arson."

15-8:   "I think we should cooperate ~~together~~."

15-9:   "I have three of those ~~in my possession~~."

15-10: "This is an improved ~~and enhanced~~ model."

Step 16

16-1:   The rain pummeled the (car's) roof ~~of the car~~.

16-2:   A (bedroom) window ~~in the bedroom~~ had been raised a few inches.

16-3:   They wandered through the (town's) streets ~~of the town~~.

16-4:   Bill lounged against the (car's) hood ~~of the car~~.

16-5:   She marched to the (van's) open passenger door ~~of the van~~.

16-6:   He was a (country) doctor ~~from the country~~.

16-7:   Please give me (that drawer's) ~~the~~ contents ~~of that drawer~~.

16-8:   It was the (show's) last skit ~~of the show~~.

16-9:   It was the (group's) largest one ~~in the group~~.

16-10: It leaned against the (house's) north wall ~~of the house~~.

Step 17

17-1:   They heard ~~the noise of~~ children in the playground.

17-2:   Debris blocked ~~off~~ the path.

17-3:   He walked ~~over~~ to the window

17-4:   "We're wondering which trails ~~we want~~ to take."

17-5:   Each ~~of them~~ wondered what would happen.

17-6:   Ahead ~~of her~~, a stocky boy sat on the diving board.

17-7: But her thoughts were a million miles away ~~at that moment~~.

17-8: The sky ~~above~~ was cloudy.

17-9: He wants to ~~try to~~ understand the problem.

17-10 He disappeared ~~from sight~~.

Step 18

18-1: The horse (was gone) ~~wasn't anywhere to be found~~.

18-2: Let's (ride alone) ~~take the horses out by ourselves~~.

18-3: She (spoke mostly) ~~directed most of her comments~~ to Lisa.

18-4: ~~His thoughts becoming jumbled,~~ Dick tuned out (his jumbled thoughts) ~~them~~.

18-5: She gathered the (pancake) ingredients ~~she needed for the pancakes~~.

18-6: (I have a short work schedule) ~~I'm only scheduled for a few hours of work~~ today.

18-7: Judy drove (aimlessly) ~~around with no destination in mind~~.

18-8: She (froze) ~~found herself unable to move~~.

18-9: (He could barely) ~~It was all he could do to~~ maintain his own energy.

18-10: Her mind was (blank) ~~devoid of any thoughts~~.

Step 19

(Note: Make up your own replacements)

19-1: The jilted bride was ~~sadder but wiser~~ _____ .

19-2: It was ~~a real shot in the arm~~ _____ .

19-3: Boy, that guy's ~~as sly as a fox~~ _____ .

19-4: Someday ~~my ship will come in~~ _____ .

19-5: That repair ~~sticks out like a sore thumb~~ _____ .

19-6: Let's ~~take the bull by the horns~~ _____ .

19-7: We've been together ~~through thick and thin~~ _____ .

19-8: Let's not ~~beat around the bush~~ _____ .

19-9: I'd say that's ~~beyond the realm of possibility~~ _____ .

19-10: He acted like ~~a bull in a china shop~~ _____ .

Step 20

20-1: ~~As you know, this~~ (This) is a Tuesday.

20-2: ~~All things considered, it's~~ (It's) not a bad choice.

20-3: ~~As a matter of fact, it's~~ (It's) bigger than the rest.

20-4: ~~As far as I'm concerned, you~~ (You) can jump off a cliff.

20-5: It's either three or four~~, as the case may be~~.

20-6: ~~For all intents and purposes, it's~~ (It's) a done deal.

20-7: ~~For your information,~~ I'm very tired.

20-8: ~~In a manner of speaking, it's~~ (It's) the biggest frog in the pond.

20-9: ~~In a very real sense, it's~~ (It's) the better of the two.

20-10: ~~In my opinion, it~~ (It) tastes great.

Step 21

21-1: Jean's ~~eyes~~ (gaze) traveled up his slim body.

21-2: He ~~had his eyes on~~ (watched) her all day.

21-3: Her ~~eyes~~ (gaze) followed him.

21-4: Her ~~eyes~~ (gaze) took them both in.

21-5: She couldn't ~~keep her eyes~~ (stop gazing at) ~~off~~ his body.

21-6: Her ~~eyes were~~ (attention was) drawn to the pictures.

21-7: He's in the eye of the storm. (no change)

21-8: The eyes of the world are upon you. (no change)

21-9: Her ~~eyes climbed~~ (gaze traveled) up his body to his face.

21-10: ~~Her eyes traveled~~ (She gazed around) the room and out the window.

SARAH'S PERILS

A heart-wrenching story of how one innocent young lady turns the tables on her evil-doing boyfriend...

and how carefully editing that story can dispel fog and make the writing clearer and more powerful.

Chapter 1 — Marked-up version

Sarah ~~started stalking~~ (stalked) toward the exit. Joe Howard could be so exasperating! He ~~was walking~~ (walked) toward her now, probably with some lame excuse for standing her up.

~~Catching~~ (He caught) up with her,~~,~~ (.) ~~he said,~~ "I'm sorry," (he said). (") I've had a rough day. Forgive me?"

Sure, she ~~started to think~~ (thought). You say "I'm sorry," and that makes everything all right. But she didn't say it out loud. She reached her car and ~~was pushing~~ (pushed) the key into the ignition(.) ~~when he~~ (He) touched her shoulder.

"Please forgive me," he ~~was saying~~ (said). "Look—~~I'm going to leave~~ I'll (leave) in a day or two. Can't we part friends?"

"Do you ~~try to~~ ruin everybody's life that way?" she said. Immediately she wished she hadn't. She was ~~being~~ too hard on him, and she knew it. Her fingers ~~started to drum~~ (drummed) the steering wheel, making little hollow sounds. Total strangers ~~began to hurry~~ (hurried) by on the sidewalk, oblivious to their argument. Her life was ~~beginning to fall~~ (falling apart), and they were only thinking about what they ~~were going to~~ (would) have for dinner. Life just wasn't fair.

Chapter 1 — Final version

Sarah stalked toward the exit. Joe Howard could be so exasperating! He walked toward her now, probably with some lame excuse for standing her up.

He caught up with her. "I'm sorry," he said. "I've had a rough day. Forgive me?"

Sure, she thought. You say "I'm sorry," and that makes everything all right. But she didn't say it out loud. She reached her car and pushed the key into the ignition. He touched her shoulder.

"Please forgive me," he said. "Look—I'll leave in a day or two. Can't we part friends?"

"Do you ruin everybody's life that way?" she said. Immediately she wished she hadn't. She was too hard on him, and she knew it. Her fingers drummed the steering wheel, making little hollow sounds. Total strangers hurried by on the sidewalk, oblivious to their argument. Her life was falling apart, and they were only thinking about what they would have for dinner. Life just wasn't fair.

Chapter 2 — Marked-up version

Joe Howard ~~had~~ jerked the passenger door open, slid into the seat, and put a slimy hand on her arm. Well, it might as well be slimy. *He* was slimy, the way he ~~was seeing~~ (saw) Judy behind her back. ~~There were~~ (She had) good reasons to feel as she did.

"You're history," she said. "I'm going to tear up every one of your pictures. ~~Every one of your letters will be thrown~~ (I'll throw every letter) into the trash."

"You've got it wrong," he said. But (he took) that hand ~~was taken~~ away. Good thing, too. ~~She was being stared at~~ (He stared at her) with ~~his~~ wide eyes.

"Are you going to get out?" She ~~had~~ started the car and ~~was now shifting~~ shifted into drive. But he just sat there.

"God, Sarah, you're something. You don't believe everything ~~told to you by~~ that crazy woman (tells you), do you? ~~She hasn't even been~~ (I haven't even) seen ~~by me~~ (her) in a week."

She thought about what he said. ~~She had been called by~~ Judy (had called her) from the hospital not an hour before, and said she and Joe were going ~~to go~~ to the dog races that night. ~~There was something that~~ (Something) didn't add up.

"You talked with her," she said. "Do you deny that?"

"Well, no. But (she called me) ~~I was called by her. There was a conversation~~ (She talked) about dogs. Dogs, Sarah. Like I have nothing better to do than watch them run around in a circle, chasing a fake rabbit."

Chapter 2 — Final version

Joe Howard jerked the passenger door open, slid into the seat, and put a slimy hand on her arm. Well, it might as well be slimy. *He* was slimy, the way he saw Judy behind her back. She had good reasons to feel as she did.

"You're history," she said. "I'm going to tear up every one of your pictures. I'll throw every letter into the trash."

"You've got it wrong," he said. But he took that hand away. Good thing, too. He stared at her with wide eyes.

"Are you going to get out?" She started the car and shifted into drive. But he just sat there.

"God, Sarah, you're something. You don't believe everything that crazy woman tells you, do you? I haven't even seen her in a week."

She thought about what he said. Judy had called from the hospital not an hour before, and said she and Joe were going to the dog races that night. Something didn't add up.

"You talked with her," she said. "Do you deny that?"

"Well, no. But she called me. She talked about dogs. Dogs, Sarah. Like I have nothing better to do than watch them run around in a circle, chasing a fake rabbit."

Chapter 3 — Marked-up version

Sarah wasn't sure what to think. ~~Joe had a~~ (Joe's) story ~~that~~ sounded ~~honest and~~ truthful, but—well, ~~would she be able to~~ (could she) believe him?

She ~~turned and~~ glanced at him and remembered the day they'd met on this very street. ~~She'd been~~ (She was) dressing a store window mannequin at Thompson's Clothing, and he ~~had~~ walked by outside, looking into the store's window. He ~~had seen~~ (saw) her and stopped—just stopped, like he'd run into a brick wall. He ~~had~~ waved and ~~he had~~ smiled.

She ~~had felt~~ (was) embarrassed. ~~Would she have been able to ignore~~ (Could she have ignored) him if she hadn't blundered and smiled back? She ~~had~~ realized that was a mistake right off. But it ~~had been~~ (was) too late to do anything about it ~~and change things~~.

When she ~~had gone~~ (went) out for lunch, there he was, leaning against the storefront. "You're gorgeous," he ~~had~~ said. "Simply gorgeous. And you did a great job on that mannequin."

Flattery, it seemed, had gotten him everywhere.

Sarah shook herself from her memories and ~~turned and~~ pulled into the street. She ~~was driving~~ (drove) south, toward her apartment building. The evening sun ~~seemed to glance~~ (glanced) off the high-rise windows into her eyes. She ~~decided to go~~ (drove) east to Long Street, and soon the sun was ~~wholly and completely~~ blocked.

"I see you've ~~decided to forgive~~ (forgiven) me," Joe said, grinning. "May I come over tonight?"

Chapter 3 — Final version

Sarah wasn't sure what to think. Joe's story sounded plausible, but—well, could she believe him?

She glanced at him, and remembered the day they'd met on this very street. She was dressing a store window mannequin at Thompson's Clothing, and he walked by outside, looking into the store's window. He saw her and stopped—just stopped, like he'd run into a brick wall. He waved and smiled.

She had felt embarrassed. Could she have ignored him if she hadn't blundered and smiled back? She realized that was a mistake right off. But it was too late to do anything about it.

When she went out for lunch there he was, leaning against the storefront. "You're gorgeous," he said. "Simply gorgeous. And you did a great job on that mannequin."

Flattery, it seemed, had gotten him everywhere.

Sarah shook herself from her memories and pulled into the street. She drove south, toward her apartment building. The evening sun glanced off the high-rise windows into her eyes. She drove east to Long Street, and soon the sun was blocked.

"I see you've forgiven me," Joe said, grinning. "May I come over tonight?"

Chapter 4 — Marked-up version

Sarah wasn't sure what to do. She ~~looked up and~~ glanced into the rearview mirror and pulled into the traffic. She ~~reached to~~ (turned) the radio ~~and turned it~~ on low and hardly heard the ~~commentator give a~~ laxative commercial. Her seat shook as Joe ~~reached out and~~ pulled himself forward.

"I'm ~~giving you a~~ warning (you)," she said. "If you're ~~telling me a lie~~ (lying), I'll never forgive you."

"Not to worry," he said.

She ~~gave him a look and saw~~ (glanced at) his face. Her heart still ~~did a flip-flop~~ (flip-flopped) every time she saw those blue eyes, that square chin. ~~He had some hair in front that~~ (Hair) curled onto his forehead, and she wanted to ~~take it and~~ gently push it back into place. If only—

The car ahead slowed, and she ~~took her foot from the floor and started to apply~~ (slowly applied) ~~pressure to~~ the brake ~~pedal~~. "I have to ~~look ahead and~~ pay attention to my driving," she mumbled. She ~~slowed to a stop~~ (stopped) at the corner and ~~sat there and~~ waited for the light to change.

That's when she saw Judy Underwood standing on the sidewalk in her stark-white nurse's uniform. Judy stepped off the curb and tapped a thick file folder on the back window. *I don't believe this, ~~Sarah was thinking~~*. *No way do I believe this.*

Joe rolled the window down. "Where've you been?" Judy asked. "I've been waiting a whole hour."

Sarah felt like slinking away. Instead, she threw the car into park and slammed her door open. "That's it!" she said. She stepped ~~on the street and got~~ out of the car.

"You!" she screamed at Judy, while pointing to the driver's seat. "Get in. You stole my boyfriend. You might as well ~~come and~~ take my car, too!"

Chapter 4 — Final version

Sarah wasn't sure what to do. She glanced into the rearview mirror and pulled into the traffic. She turned the radio on low, and hardly heard the laxative commercial. Her seat shook as Joe pulled himself forward.

"I'm warning you," she said. "If you're lying, I'll never forgive you."

"Not to worry," he said.

She glanced at his face. Her heart still flip-flopped every time she saw those blue eyes, that square chin. Hair curled onto his forehead, and she wanted to gently push it back into place. If only—

The car ahead slowed, and she slowly applied the brake. "I have to pay attention to my driving," she said. She stopped at the corner and waited for the light to change.

That's when she saw Judy Underwood standing on the sidewalk in her stark-white nurse's uniform. Judy stepped off the curb and tapped a thick file folder on the back window. *I don't believe this. No way do I believe this.*

Joe rolled the window down. "Where've you been?" Judy asked. "I've been waiting a whole hour."

Sarah felt like slinking away. Instead, she threw the car into park and slammed her door open. "That's it!" she said. She stepped out of the car.

"You!" she screamed at Judy, while pointing to the driver's seat. "Get in. You stole my boyfriend. You might as well take my car, too!"

Chapter 5 — Marked-up version

Sarah stalked down the street. ~~She felt that~~ Joe had betrayed her. ~~She saw him running~~. (He ran) after her.

(He stopped) in front of her, out of breath. "Sarah, you don't understand," he ~~was saying, pleadingly~~ (said).

She paused, ~~saw him stop~~. "No, you're the one who doesn't ~~seem to~~ understand," she ~~yelled~~ (said). "~~I think you're~~ (You're) the most despicable person I've ever met."

~~She saw a~~ (A) car ~~stop~~ (stopped) behind hers and ~~heard~~ its horn (sounded). "~~I think you'd~~ (You'd) better move Judy's new car," she said, tossing the car keys at him. ~~She saw them bounce~~ (They bounced) off his chest.

"~~I see you~~ (You) don't understand," he said~~, plaintively~~.

"Understand what?" ~~She felt her guard go~~ (Her guard went) up. Was this another trick(?)~~, she wondered.~~

"Of course, you don't," he (said) ~~mumbled~~. "I didn't tell you."

~~She could hear more~~ (More) honking (sounded). ~~She saw a~~ (A) half dozen cars were now stacked up behind hers.

"~~I think this~~ (This) is one of your tricks," she said.

"No, I swear." ~~She felt him put his hands on~~ (He touched) her shoulder. "I just learned I have cancer. Judy's my doctor's nurse. That dog-racing business—she was just trying to take my mind off the cancer."

~~Sarah could see he~~ (He) was serious. "Well, I don't know," she said~~, thoughtfully~~.

"~~I think you~~ (You) should come back and ask her yourself," he said.

Chapter 5 — Final version

Sarah stalked down the street. Joe had betrayed her. He ran after her.

He stopped in front of her, out of breath. "Sarah, you don't understand," he said.

She paused. "No, you're the one who doesn't understand," she said. "You're the most despicable person I've ever met."

A car stopped behind hers and its horn sounded. "You'd better move Judy's new car," she said, tossing the car keys at him. They bounced off his chest.

"You don't understand," he said.

"Understand what?" Her guard went up. Was this another trick.

"Of course, you don't," he said. "I didn't tell you."

More honking sounded. A half dozen cars were now stacked up behind hers.

"This is one of your tricks," she said.

"No, I swear." He touched her shoulder. "I just learned I have cancer. Judy's my doctor's nurse. That dog-racing business—she was just trying to take my mind off the cancer."

He was serious. "Well, I don't know," she said.

"You should come back and ask her yourself," he said.

Chapter 6 — Marked-up version

Sarah stared at Joe. "I don't know whether to believe you or not(.)~~,~~" ~~she said, a touch of doubt in her voice. "A part of me wants to, but some things don't seem to add up. Am I to really believe you have cancer? It would seem to me that you would have told me about that sooner, and not wait until now. Why, if you really do have it, that's awful. I—"~~

(His eyebrows raised.) "Why shouldn't you believe me(?)~~,~~" ~~he said, questioningly.~~ "Look—I'm dying of cancer. Why would I ~~want to~~ lie?"

"Well, I don't believe it(.)~~,~~" (She crossed her arms and stared at the ground.) ~~she said, thinking he was probably lying.~~

He took her hand. "Come ask Judy~~," he said in a pleading way~~. "She'll tell you."

"I—I guess it couldn't hurt(.)~~,~~" ~~she said hesitantly.~~ She ~~started following~~ (followed) him toward her car. Judy, standing by the door, appeared nervous.

"I told her about my cancer," Joe said. "You know—the cancer you came to tell me about?"

Judy stared blankly at him for several seconds(.)~~, obviously thinking about what he said~~. "The—the cancer?" ~~she said, after a pause.~~

"The cancer you came to tell me about~~, remember?" he said, almost repeating himself~~. "I told Sarah you were just giving me more information about it."

"Oh, *that* cancer!" Judy said, reaching out and touching Sarah's arm. "That's what the doctor said."

(Sarah glanced at Joe.) "Oh, goodness~~," Sarah started to say~~. ~~"~~Joe, I'm so sorry."

Wait. Something was amiss. Something about Judy's hand....

(Joe caught her stare and looked up.) "Is something wrong?" ~~Joe said.~~

That—that ring on Judy's hand! "Oh, I see it all now~~," she said, as if she realized something~~. "Joe—that's your ring!"

Chapter 6 — Final version

Sarah stared at Joe. "I don't know whether to believe you or not."

His eyebrows raised. "Why shouldn't you believe me? Look—I'm dying of cancer. Why would I lie?"

"Well, I don't believe it." She crossed her arms and stared at the ground.

He took her hand. "Come ask Judy. She'll tell you."

"I—I guess it couldn't hurt." She followed him to her car. Judy, standing by the door, appeared nervous.

"I told her about my cancer," Joe said. "You know—the cancer you came to tell me about?"

Judy stared blankly at him for several seconds. "The—the cancer?"

"The cancer you came to tell me about, remember? I told Sarah you were just giving me more information about it."

"Oh, *that* cancer!" Judy touched Sarah's arm. "That's what the doctor said."

Sarah glanced at Joe. "Oh, goodness. Joe, I'm so sorry."

Wait. Something was amiss. Something about Judy's hand....

Joe caught her stare and looked up. "Is something wrong?"

That—that ring on Judy's hand! "Oh, I see it all now. Joe—that's your ring!"

Chapter 7 — Marked-up version

Anger warmed ~~the cheeks of~~ Sarah's ~~face~~ (cheeks). She ~~put the palm of her hand on~~ (grabbed) the (opened) door~~, which was open,~~ for support.

Joe ~~said,~~ (pursed his lips.) "Well, what really happened, was—"

She slid into the driver's seat. "Forget it, Joe. You two get away from my car!"

Judy ~~moved away from the car and~~ stepped onto the ~~edge of the~~ sidewalk, and Joe slammed the door ~~of the car~~ closed. "You don't know what you're doing, Sarah. The doctor said I have cancer of the lungs."

"Right." ~~Sarah had a~~ (Her) head ~~that~~ throbbed, and ~~a~~ (her) boyfriend ~~who~~ was ~~being~~ unfaithful. Which was worse?

Sarah slammed the gearshift home and screeched out. She turned left at the next corner ~~of the street~~, swerving to miss (oncoming) traffic ~~coming her way~~. That Joe ~~was going to~~ (would) get his, she fumed. He—

Her cell phone rang, and she jumped. She opened it ~~and spoke into the mouthpiece~~. "Hello?"

"It's me." Joe's voice. "Don't hang up! Can I trust you?"

"What?"

"I need to talk with you about something of importance to the nation. It has to do with the CIA. I'll be at your place at eight this evening. Be there."

He hung up~~, ending the conversation~~.

Chapter 7 — Final version

Anger warmed Sarah's cheeks. She grabbed the opened door for support.

Joe pursed his lips. "Well, what really happened, was—"

She slid into the driver's seat. "Forget it, Joe. You two get away from my car!"

Judy stepped onto the sidewalk, and Joe slammed the door closed. "You don't know what you're doing, Sarah. The doctor said I have cancer of the lungs."

"Right." Her head throbbed, and her boyfriend was unfaithful. Which was worse?

Sarah slammed the gearshift home and screeched out. She turned left at the next corner, swerving to miss oncoming traffic. That Joe would get his, she fumed. He—

Her cell phone rang, and she jumped. She opened it. "Hello?"

"It's me." Joe's voice. "Don't hang up! Can I trust you?"

"What?"

"I need to talk with you about something of importance to the nation. It has to do with the CIA. I'll be at your place at eight this evening. Be there."

He hung up.

Chapter 8 — Marked-up version

Sarah slammed the cell phone onto the seat. Damn him! She switched on the radio, and the loud rock-and-roll music ~~from it seemed to be making~~ (made) her even more agitated. She (sighed) ~~let out a sigh~~. Even the traffic was ~~as busy as Grand Central Station~~ (terrible). She turned left ~~on the other side of~~ (beyond) the mall to avoid it.

The car ~~in the road~~ ahead ~~of her suddenly~~ stopped ~~at the blink of an eye~~ (abruptly), (and she braked hard). ~~Too late, she took her foot off the accelerator and put it on the brake, and pressed hard.~~ Her car skidded ~~on the road beneath her~~ and ~~her car~~ tapped the other's rear bumper. She (tensed) ~~felt her body go tense~~.

(She glanced at) ~~Her eyes moved over~~ the other car. Apparently, no damage. "Sorry," she called out, as she pulled around it. That damned, lying Joe!

She pondered the ~~meaning of~~ the phone call. Important to the nation? (What did that mean?) ~~She needed to try to understand what he meant.~~ (Why,) ~~She was starting to think that~~ he was being dishonest ~~with her~~. Joe, Joe, my boy. You're full of it. But I'll get even. You—

And then it hit her~~, like a bolt from the blue~~. The perfect solution. ~~After all, all was fair in love and war.~~

She arrived at her apartment building, pulled into her assigned (parking) spot ~~in the parking area~~, ~~got out~~, and ~~soon she~~ was (soon) in her eighth floor apartment.

Meet her here at eight, huh? Well, okay.

~~Cool as a cucumber, she~~ (She calmly) ~~walked over to the phone and~~ picked ~~it~~ up (the phone) and dialed the number for Thompson's Clothing.

Chapter 8 — Final version

Sarah slammed the cell phone onto the seat. Damn him! She switched on the radio, and the loud rock-and-roll music made her even more agitated. She sighed. Even the traffic was terrible. She turned left beyond the mall to avoid it.

The car ahead stopped abruptly, and she braked hard. Her car skidded and tapped the other's rear bumper. She tensed.

She glanced at the other car. Apparently, no damage. "Sorry," she called out, as she pulled around it. That damned, lying Joe!

She pondered the phone call. Important to the nation? What did that mean? Why, he was being dishonest. Joe, Joe, my boy. You're full of it. But I'll get even. You—

And then it hit her. The perfect solution.

She arrived at her apartment building, pulled into her assigned parking spot, and was soon in her eighth floor apartment.

Meet her here at eight, huh? Well, okay.

She calmly picked up the phone and dialed the number for Thompson's Clothing.

Chapter 9 — Marked-up version

Sarah licked the pencil tip. Revenge, sweet revenge. ~~Then she~~ (She) put her pencil to the paper and wrote the message: *Joe. The door's unlocked. I have a surprise for you.*

She signed her name, ~~then got some tape and~~ taped the note on the outside of her apartment door(, and). ~~She suddenly looked~~ (glanced) at her watch. ~~She knew that~~ Joe would be there soon. She just had one more note to write. She (sat at) ~~went to~~ the table ~~that was~~ by the open balcony door and ~~sat at it and~~ wrote bold letters on a large piece of paper.

~~Suddenly the~~ (The) elevator door clicked in the hall. She dropped the paper on the carpet by the hall door and ~~then~~ ran into the bedroom. ~~Her eyes traveled~~ (She peered) back through the crack between the door and the jamb. ~~Suddenly,~~ Joe opened the door and entered.

"Sarah?" He ~~looked~~ (frowned) down ~~and saw~~ (at) the note, ~~and then he frowned. He~~ picked it up and read it, and slumped. "Oh, God(.)~~,~~" ~~he was saying~~. He ~~started to walk toward the balcony, and then he~~ ran out onto (the balcony)~~it~~.

Sarah counted. *One, two, three...*

"Sarah!~~" he suddenly screamed.~~ "God, what did I do?"

|Silence. ~~Then he came back in and just kept walking until he was~~ (He walked back through the apartment and) out the hall door. Moments later, the elevator clicked.

~~It went without saying that he~~ (He) was gone from her life forever.

Sarah ~~then~~ went into the living room and picked up the note. She ~~was smiling~~ (smiled) as she read it: *"I'm tired of your un-faithfulness. I'm going to jump off the balcony."*

She ~~suddenly~~ walked out onto the balcony and ~~her eyes hit~~ (stared down at) the ground. ~~In the final analysis, the~~ (The) store mannequin did look real. Especially the way its arms and legs were twisted every which way.

Gotcha, Joey baby.

Chapter 9 — Final version

Sarah licked the pencil tip. Revenge, sweet revenge. She put her pencil to the paper and wrote the message: *Joe. The door's unlocked. I have a surprise for you.*

She signed her name, taped the note on the outside of her apartment door, and glanced at her watch. Joe would be there soon. She just had one more note to write. She sat at the table by the open balcony door and wrote bold letters on a large piece of paper.

The elevator door clicked in the hall. She dropped the paper on the carpet by the hall door and ran into the bedroom. She peered back through the crack between the door and the jamb. Joe opened the door and entered.

"Sarah?" He frowned down at the note, picked it up and read it, and slumped. "Oh, God." He ran out onto the balcony.

Sarah counted. *One, two, three...*

"Sarah! God, what did I do?"

Silence. He walked back through the apartment and out the hall door. Moments later, the elevator clicked.

He was gone from her life forever.

Sarah went into the living room and picked up the note. She smiled as she read it: *"I'm tired of your unfaithfulness. I'm going to jump off the balcony."*

She walked out onto the balcony and stared down at the ground. The store mannequin did look real. Especially the way its arms and legs were twisted every which way.

Gotcha, Joey baby.

Mystery on Firefly Knob
Synopsis

Erica Philips, a single, twenties-something Glen Ellyn, Illinois, antiques dealer who must soon vacate her store due to urban blight, receives a registered letter from Crossville, Tennessee, lawyer Charles Connors. He says her deceased father, Patrick Emerson, was killed while felling a tree on his property and has willed her a rustic cabin and two hundred acres atop the Cumberland Plateau's Rymer's Knob.

But wait—her father was Paul Phillips. And he was killed in an auto accident in Crystal Lake, Illinois, four years ago!

Erica drives to Connors's Crossville offices, where she learns Emerson fathered her in high school, and her mother married Paul before giving birth. Connors gives her the cabin's keys and a scribbled map and tells her a condo builder is interested in buying the property. She says she'll sell it and use the money to acquire a new building for her antiques business.

When Erica arrives at her new property she finds a small 1930s log cabin and a decrepit carriage house overlooking Sequatchie Valley, eighteen hundred feet below her and stretching south for many miles. She's surprised by Mike Cleverdon, a thirty-year-old college professor and Oak Ridge National Laboratories scientist who's camping there to study rare "synchronous" fireflies, so named because they flash simultaneously. He's agitated to learn she may sell the land to a condo builder, who would undoubtedly ruin the firefly habitat. She is defiant. "If I have my way, this place will be sold within the week," she tells him. "And, Mr. Cleverdon, I *will* have my way!"

Condo builder Peter Donovan and his driver, Bruce Littinghouse, arrive that afternoon to discuss buying the property, and Mike interrupts their meeting. Miffed, Erica acts as if she's signing a sales offer, while she's actually only making whispered plans for the builder to take necessary core samples within two days. Later that day she visits Mike's camp, and they discover a mutual attraction. He impulsively kisses her.

Erica thinks about that kiss the next day at lawyer Connors' office, as she signs the papers to transfer the deed from her father's estate to her. She returns to the Knob to find grad students installing cameras and scientific equipment. Mike says the fireflies will hatch in a week or two. Erica asks her antique shop assistant, via the Knob's on-again, off-again cell phone service, to price a Glen Ellyn shoe store building as a possible new business site. She's to run a March of Dimes 10K race there on Saturday and may make an offer then, pending the sale of her father's property. When she and Mike view the felled tree with her father's friend Paul Rothert, a retired New York City police detective, he points out clues which show her father might have been murdered. She and Mike visit the coroner's office to pick up a coroner's report and death scene pictures.

The next day Mike, resigned to losing the research site to condos, takes her on an impromptu picnic hike to the property's original 1800s cabin site, situated on the steep cliff several hundred feet away from the current cabin. They discover a pioneer cemetery behind the old cabin's stone foundation and feel very romantic—that is, until Erica reminds him of the imminent condo development sale. The bubble bursts, and he takes her back to her cabin.

Earthmovers invade the cabin's clearing two days later and erect a derrick-like drill. Mike pleads with Erica to send them away before they change the fireflies' patterns. When she explains they must take core samples before buying the property he realizes she didn't sign that sales contract after all, that she was playing mind games with him. This was war! He storms back to his camp and makes several telephone calls.

Erica runs her foot race in Glen Ellyn that weekend and is confronted by a wire-service reporter who tells her a "fireflies" article on her property will appear nationally in Monday's daily papers. That darned Mike! She realizes she must talk with her mom before she reads that article. She visits her mom, announces she knows Emerson was her father, and asks, "Momma—Momma, did Daddy know?" To her relief, he did. Her tearful mom explains both men loved Erica dearly; that Patrick vowed to stay out of her life but was always there in spirit; that he sent her anonymous gifts, attended many of her school functions, even talked a maiden aunt into hiring her summers to work in her antiques shop. The woman eventually left her antiques business to Erica in her will, at the behest of Patrick Emerson.

Erica returns to the Tennessee cabin, where Mike apologizes for his impulsive actions with a room full of flowers. But it's too late to return the genie to the bottle, and the article appears in the papers the next day. Donovan makes another offer and Mike tops it; he's started a "Dollars from Scholars" fund that encourages university faculty and students throughout the U.S. to pledge money to buy the property and establish a national "Firefly Knob" study site. Mike says he'll ask his father, "Bull" Cleverdon, a former minor league sports personality and founder and longtime owner of a popular Knoxville sports brewpub, to provide interim financing until the pledges come in. He and his father are virtually estranged because, in his father's eyes, Mike fell short of his high school and college athletic potential and became an "egghead" instead. His older brother, a star athlete until he was killed in an auto accident, remains his father's favorite son.

Mike takes Erica to his Oak Ridge National Laboratory (ORNL) office that afternoon so she can use his Internet account to research her father online. Mike's boss, Martin Sherman, tells her he plans to acquire her property for the government by eminent domain. Furious with Mike, who insists he didn't know of that "eminent domain" plan, Erica makes him take her back to the Knob. They arrive at dark and she refuses to go up to the cabin on the back of his ATV; he goes up alone. When she attempts to jog up in the gloom she loses her footing and falls, breaking her leg and knocking herself unconscious. He finds her still unconscious the next morning and takes her to the Knoxville hospital, where she will spend the night.

Mike goes to his father's brewpub to ask for interim financing, and his father turns him down. He tells Mike to not rock the boat; he has a good job, and he's the obvious person to run the firefly program after the government takes over Erica's property. Mike asks to borrow his mother's wheelchair, gathering dust since her death from leukemia two years before.

The next day at the hospital Mike asks Erica to let him and his students care for her as she recuperates at the cabin; it's impossible for her to drive home to northern Illinois, let alone take care of herself when she got there. He explains his father won't loan him the interim money, but promises he will somehow keep his ORNL boss from taking her land by eminent domain. They return to the cabin, where she asks him to roll her wheelchair over to the downed tree that killed her father. There she looks at the site and the pictures from the coroner's office and realizes, as Paul Rothert surmised, that the death was not an accident. "Mike, my father wasn't killed cutting this tree down," she says. "My father was murdered."

As proof she points out her father was lying face up across the path of the fallen tree rather than parallel to it; if it were an accident, the tree would have fallen lengthwise on him. Also, there's a smear of blood a foot from where his head was. After that tree fell on him there was no way he could have moved that foot's length. He had to have been dragged at least that distance before the tree hit him. Her conclusion, after studying the coroner's report, the death scene pictures, and her father's computer appointment calendar? "Mike, the murderers are… Mr. Donovan the condo man and his driver Bruce Littinghouse!" She theorizes that Donovan couldn't get him to sell the property and thought he'd have an easier time convincing his heir… her.

Mike agrees. Now they must find the murder weapon, or they have little chance of proving murder. Mike and his grad students scour the property for a thrown-away bloody club or other weapon, but find nothing. Thinking the weapon might be in the back of Donovan's truck, they hatch an idea; while Erica stalls Donovan and his driver on the cabin's porch on their next visit, Mike will search their truck. Shortly before they arrive, she calls lawyer Connors to tell him their theories and their plan to expose the murderers. He cautions her to be careful, just as her erratic cell phone service is interrupted. An hour later, at dusk, the condo people arrive.

Erica and Mike work their plan until Donovan's driver hears Mike rummaging through the truck's bed behind the cabin. He stalks around the building, followed by Donovan, and confronts Mike, who has found a bloody crowbar. Erica grabs an old flintlock rifle from over the fireplace, hobbles after them, and sees them approaching Mike. She points the useless weapon at them and tells them to stop. Two shots ring out, and both Donovan and his driver drop dead. Someone—a third party, unknown—has killed them!

Other shots ring out and Mike grabs Erica. He places her on the back of his ATV and starts down the Knob's trail, hopefully to safety. Another shot is fired from down the hill. He pauses. His grad students would be in danger if he went their direction. He drives a third direction—to the original cabin site and its pioneer cemetery. He carries Erica across the open area and lays her among the old tombstones. Darkness is complete, except for an occasional glimmer from the moon as the clouds move. He inches back to his ATV as he hears the killer arrive on foot.

Erica is desperate to get help. She can't open her cell phone for fear that its bright glow would give the killer a target. If she holds the phone tightly to her face to block the light, she can't see her cell phone's buttons and therefore can't easily dial. But she realizes if she presses the "send" button twice—she can locate it by feel—it will dial the last number she'd spoken to. She punches the button, praying the intermittent phone service would work, and that lawyer Connors will pick up. After moments the phone rings… both in the cell phone she holds to her ear, and on the Knob itself. The implication hits her hard. She calls out. "Mike—Mike, that's Mr. Connors shooting at us!"

Mike hears her shouted message just as he reaches his ATV. He revs its motor and turns on its headlights in time to see Connors, poised on the rocky ledge overlooking Sequatchie Valley, aim his pistol at Erica. Conners takes several quick shots at her, all the time sobbing and saying it was her fault, that if she'd just sold the property like she was supposed to and gone home, everything would have been fine… but she made him kill Donovan and Littinghouse so they wouldn't implicate him in the Emerson killing, and now he had to kill her and Mike. The slugs career off rocks and tombstones and into trees, dangerously close to Erica. As the clouds shift and moonlight briefly appears, he sets himself for a careful aim at her, now starkly evident in the little cemetery. Mike jams the accelerator and aims the ATV for Connors, who jumps back to avoid it, and falls backwards over the cliff into the Sequatchie Valley below.

Mike helps Erica to the old cabin's foundation. They sit silently, where they had earlier picnicked, peering out into beautiful Sequatchie Valley and holding each other closely. She realizes how much she loves him. As they watch points of light which mark the little farm home windows below, she becomes aware of closer lights. Something blinks in the grass. Another blink, then another. Soon the area is awash with blinking points of light. As they watch, the independent blinks of newly-hatched fireflies meld into one, and the light moves in waves, up and down Rymer's Knob. Within seconds, all the lights flash off and on in unison. Erica's eyes tear, and she hugs Mike. She is overwhelmed by the moment's beauty.

The next day at the main cabin, Erica tells Mike she has a surprise. They walk to the site's decrepit carriage house, and she tells him that will be her new antique shop. She's moving to the site, and will not disturb the fireflies' habitat with massive earthmoving and building. She and Mike express their lifelong commitment to each other.

A year later, Erica drives her van up the newly surfaced road to the cabin site and parks. She follows the "Firefly Knob" arrow around the cabin on a plank walk and notes visitors at the cliff's edge, peering out at the spectacular view next to the "Sequatchie Valley Overlook" sign. She enters the busy Firefly Knob Antiques shop and learns from her assistant that Mike has just returned from his father's house in Knoxville. Mike had bridged the gap between himself and his father, who had a heart attack and subsequently a change of heart, realizing his older son was a strong man in his own way. She's pleased Mike's home, since she has a surprise for him.

She finds him and leads him off the paved road to the original cabin site, which now features the brand new log cabin they've just moved into. She tells him they are having a one-year anniversary picnic in the rock foundation of the vintage cabin. As he goes into the house to get a blanket she walks to the pioneer cemetery a few feet away in the woods, where her father's body was recently buried after being exhumed to prove he was indeed murdered. Her research had shown that the bare foundation was that of Edmund Rymer's very own cabin, built in the early 1800s, soon after he moved his family to this wilderness outpost. This was his family cemetery. She had traced Emerson's family tree—her family tree—back to Rymer. She kneels at her father's grave. Her biological father was now near her. She returns to the picnic site, where Mike has just arrived, and says, "I have a surprise. I didn't happen to mention this morning that I'd just learned I'm pregnant, did I?"

A stunned look appears on his face, and turns into one of joy. He pulls her down so she's flat on her back, and tenderly kisses her. "You've just made my day," he says. "No, make that my life."

He kisses her again, and she glows as she returns it. Her father, her home, her husband, her baby… her life was finally complete.

Novels used as examples

The following novels, used as examples throughout this book, are available from Amazon.com, BarnesandNoble.com, and other online digital book companies.

Mystery on Firefly Knob

The Long Hunter

Attack of the Killer Prom Dresses

Mystery at Magnolia Mansion

BJ, Milo, and the Hairdo from Heck

Waiting for Backup!

Index

More Great Books for Writers from Quill Driver Books

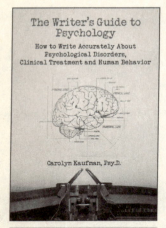

$14.95 ($16.95 Canada)

The Writer's Guide to Psychology

How to Write Accurately About Psychological Disorders, Clinical Treatment and Human Behavior

by Carolyn Kaufman, Psy.D.

Written by a clinical psychologist who is also a professional writer and writing coach, *The Writer's Guide to Psychology* is an authoritative and easy-to-use reference to psychological disorders, diagnosis, treatments, and what really makes psychopathic villains tick. The only reference book on psychology written specifically for writers, *The Writer's Guide to Psychology* presents specific writing dos and don'ts to avoid the misunderstandings frequently seen in popular writing.

$14.95 ($16.95 Canada)

Agatha Award Winner
Best Nonfiction Book

Books, Crooks and Counselors

How to Write Accurately About Criminal Law and Courtroom Procedure

by Leslie Budewitz, mystery writer and attorney at law

Books, Crooks and Counselors is an easy-to-use, practical, and reliable guide book that shows writers how to use the law to create fiction that is accurate, true to life and crackling with real-world tension ad conflict. Leslie Budewitz, a mystery writer and practicing lawyer with over 25 year of courtroom experience, will teach you the facts of legal procedure, what lawyers and judges really think about the law, and authentic courtroom dialogue.